A disequilibrium analysis of the labour market

Disequilibrium on the labour market is not only relevant for wage formation, but implies that employment and labour force are only by coincidence equal to anticipated labour demand and supply. This study demonstrates the feasibility of an iterative estimation of ex ante demand and supply. The estimation procedure combines conventional demand and supply analysis (production-models, population growth, wage development etc.) with rather appealing assumptions about the economics of disequilibrium. This approach is applied to the Dutch labour market. However, it proves relevant for theoretical and empirical macro-economic model building in general.

A disequilibrium analysis of the labour market

R. S. G. Lenderink and
J. C. Siebrand

Rotterdam University Press/1976

Printed in the Netherlands

ISBN 90 237 2277 9

Preface

We started this study in the summer of 1972. It seemed a natural follow-up to our earlier research activities. Lenderink was engaged in a study of the labour supply in the Netherlands, Siebrand had just finished a disequilibrium analysis of Dutch foreign trade. The first empirical results of our joint attempts to apply the same linear disequilibrium model to the Dutch labour market confirmed some of the basic notions. However, on the whole the results did not come up to our expectations.
This failure led in 1973 to the development of a more general, non-linear, analysis of disequilibrium, which proved to be more successful. After some reshaping of the labour demand and supply analysis the empirical work was finished in 1974. The final version of this study was completed in 1975.
This work contains several, more or less separated, subjects. In its preparation we applied a certain division of labour. The derivation of potential employment on the basis of the production function is basically Lenderink's work. Siebrand provided the disequilibrium analysis. Most other parts are the result of close cooperation. Of course, both of us accept the responsibility for the entire text.
We are indebted to a number of people. Prof.Dr. F.W. Rutten showed great interest in our work; his encouragement and comments, especially in the earlier stages of the gestation period of this book were a great support for us. We are very grateful to Mr. A. Knoester and Mr. V.R. Okker for their devoted and able assistance on all levels of activity. Our special gratitude is due to Mr. W.C. Verbaan who patiently provided all required computer programs and to Mr. W.J. Keller who designed an elegant mathematical formulation for

the distribution of disequilibrium over demand and supply. Special recognition is also due to Mrs. E.G. Bontenbal-Schuiten and Mrs. J.A. van den Bandt-Stel for typing out the manuscript several times with changing enthusiasm but constant accuracy. Finally we would like to express our special gratitude also to Dr. R. Bathgate, who corrected the English of the final text.

Rotterdam, August 1975

Contents

List of appendices

1. Introduction

In current macro-economics there is a peculiar dichotomy in the use of the equilibrium assumption with regard to the labour market. Wage theory usually assumes disequilibrium, but as a rule the analysis of employment and labour supply is implicitly based on equilibrium. Both traditions are historically understandable, but their combination seems hardly acceptable. This study discards with the less general and therefore less defendable of the two traditions: our analysis of labour demand and labour supply is explicitly based on the disequilibrium assumption. This does not imply that we had to do away with all achievements of equilibrium labour market analysis. On the contrary, our approach integrates the conventional analysis with the formalisation of the consequences of disequilibrium.
In our study, as in many other labour market studies, the labour supply is related to population growth while labour demand is derived from the production function. This production function assumes complementarity of capital and labour per vintage; hence, the labour required for the operation of the new capital goods is directly related to investment. The technical production capacity is not always fully utilized; its operating rate depends partly on (volume) demand for products, partly on the extent to which (variable) labour costs are covered by product revenue. Technical deterioration of capital causes a loss of jobs. In the short run, imperfect divisibility of labour leads to (implicit) variations in overtime; in the longer run the decrease of contractual working time is assumed to cause a proportional increase in jobs. Effective machine-operating time is related to contractual working hours. An impact of business liquidity on labour demand separate from the production function

is postulated.
Studies of labour supply often break down active population into several groups. In our analysis, such a division is used only for an approximation of the partial effects of the changes in the population composition on macro labour supply. Changes in labour-force participation caused by changes in real wages per hour and changes connected with time are dealt with in an overall way. Both impacts are related to the level of participation in such a way that they fade away when participation reaches its saturation level. External labour migration is linked to the determinants of domestic labour supply. Short-term fluctuations in labour supply caused by changes in the tension on the labour market, the 'discouraged worker' effect, are introduced as a typical disequilibrium phenomenon.
The direct implication of the disequilibrium assumption for the labour market is that actual employment and actual labour supply are only by coincidence equal to intended (or expected) labour demand and intended labour supply respectively. In line with prominent studies on disequilibrium it is argued that conventional demand and supply analysis deals with these potential (notional) entities. If this is true there exists a theoretical and empirical gap between realisations and demand and supply theory.
The obvious obstacle for research in terms of ex ante (potential) entities is of course the lack of reliable data. Perhaps this is the main reason why disequilibrium is much more often invoked in theoretical than in empirical studies.
In principle, this bottleneck could be removed by gaining accurate direct information on the expectations and intentions of economic subjects. However, in the absence of such information it is possible and worth-while to undertake an indirect approach, as this study shows.
In a theoretical discussion of the disequilibrium labour market we argue that the short side of the market by itself may not always dominate actual transactions. More specifically, our arguments lead to functional dependence of actual labour demand and actual labour

supply on both potential labour demand and potential labour supply.

Differentiation of this dependence with respect to time yields expressions for the changes in actual labour demand and actual labour supply in terms of levels and changes of the potential variables. These expressions form the basis for an iterative estimation procedure in which more and more _ex post_ entities are gradually replaced by their potential counterparts. The determination of potential labour demand and potential labour supply follows the 'equilibrium-theory' lines explained above.

The theoretical labour market model is developed in chapter 2. Chapter 3 describes the estimation procedure. Chapter 4 contains an elaborate derivation of industry's potential labour demand. The vintage production function is introduced in 4.1.1. The analysis of potential labour supply in chapter 5 refers to the dependent labour population. Chapter 6 combines the elements discussed previously in one operational model. This model is applied to Dutch data for the period 1952-1970 in chapter 7. This chapter offers among other things an interesting interpretation of the deterioration of the employment situation during the sixties in the Netherlands. Moreover, the values of potential and actual labour supply and demand are compared.
Chapter 8 comments briefly on the implications of the present study for further research. Chapter 9 contains a summary.

2. The labour market in disequilibrium[1]

There seems to be abundant empirical evidence for the relevance of disequilibrium to the labour market. The registration of the unemployed, i.e. people unable to find work (at the prevailing wage rates), clearly points in this direction. Information from various industrial countries over the past few decades suggests that periods of labour shortage can occur, in spite of labour imports and temporarily rising participation rates generated by tension on the labour market. While part of these disequilibria may be due to the heterogeneous character of the labour market, empirical information does indicate that it may be worth-while to specify the possibilities of excess demand and excess supply in a simplified aggregated analysis of the short-run phenomena on the labour market.

At a theoretical level, the present state of affairs with regard to the disequilibrium analysis of the labour market is somewhat fragmentary.
Keynes' General Theory certainly made many economists become interested in the relevance of excess supply of labour in the current sense of the term.[2]

The unemployment rate as the most obvious indicator of excess supply

---

1. Numbers between{ } refer to the list of references.
2. It is noteworthy that Keynes himself limited the concept of 'involuntary unemployment' to what might be described as a non-optimality property of an economic system: the simultaneous rise of labour supply and labour demand to a higher level than that of actual employment, as a result of a small increase in the profit margin on the commodity market (cf. {20} pp. 15 and 26).

of labour plays a dominant role in the empirical construction of macro-economic models initiated in the late thirties by J. Tinbergen and R. Frisch. A somewhat different line of development is connected with the name of A.W. Phillips.[1] The macro-economic theory of wage determination explicitly takes diseouilibrium on the labour market as a starting point. A third, more recent theoretical development based on the work of Keynes and relevant for empirical short-run analysis of the labour market is what might be called the general theory of disequilibrium. Clower {8}, Patinkin {30}, Leijonhufvud {25}, Grossman and Barro {4}, among others, have worked in this field.

More or less separate from this line of development, but also important for disequilibrium analysis, is the work of authors such as Kornai {24}, who strongly disapproves of the habit of assuming equilibrium, Nelson and Winter {29}, who are trying to develop an evolutionary theory of firm behaviour, Alchian {1} who stresses the relevance of information costs and other writers on search theory.

Although a number of empirical disequilibrium studies have emerged of recent years, the empirical implementation of disequilibrium theory is still in the take-off stage.

One of the objectives of this report is to provide a link between 'traditional' macro-economic model building and more rigid disequilibrium analysis. In the absence of reliable <u>ex ante</u> data, this requires 1) formulation of a disequilibrium theory explicit enough to serve as a basis for an estimation procedure and 2) development of an estimation procedure for the approximation of <u>ex ante</u> variables.

The first step will be elaborated in this chapter, and the second in chapter 3.

Any disequilibrium theory has to deal with excess demand and/or excess supply, situations in which sellers or buyers cannot trade

---

1) A.W. Phillips {32}; B. Hansen {16} points out, however, that Tinbergen used a linear Phillips relation as early as 1936.

the quantities they want to at the prevailing prices: prices are rigid, or at least not so flexible that demand and supply can reach complete equality.
Demand or supply surplusses generally generate adaptation processes that tend to decrease these surplusses. It is therefore meaningful to differentiate (at least) between the initial (ex ante) situation and the final (ex post) situation.
The next problem is the simultaneous introduction of ex ante and ex post entities in one operational model. The economic literature offers hardly any examples of such models. The bulk of empirical macro-economic studies are limited to actual entities, representing ex post situations. On the other hand data on expectations and aims are collected on a large scale, and these ex ante data are frequently used in the explanation of the actual state of affairs; however, problems like the origin of expectations[1] and the confrontation of aims with the possibilities of realizing them have received relatively little investigation.
To clear a way through the field of (ex ante) intentions, an operational definition of ex ante aims is essential.
On a theoretical level, the work of Patinkin and Clower offers points of contact with our approach. Patinkin ({30},p.314) uses the supply curve of labour as the norm of reference for the definition of involuntary unemployment. Clower ({8}, p. 116) seems to have the same theory in mind when he defines notional demand (supply) as equilibrium demand (supply) according to conventional demand (supply) analysis. The present analysis links up with the ex ante concepts of these authors. In its empirical application, it bears some similarity to a study of Gregory {13} and earlier work of the second author {33}.
To explain our approach we have to go briefly into disequilibrium economics. The adaptation of economic behaviour to external circum-

1. Cf. L. Klein {21}.

stances is a time-consuming and costly process. An essential complication in this context is the uncertainty of future developments. Economic subjects may base their behaviour on expectations; they may also try to avoid or limit risks. It seems in general appropriate to assume that - beyond a certain limit - uncertainty increases with the length of the period involved. A similar relationship may exist between adaptation possibilities and period length. Hence, optimalisation means different things for different periods; and lagged reactions to short-term behaviour may conflict with long-term aims. Conversely, long-term intentions may constitute a constraint for short-term behaviour; in other words, long-term rationality may lead to sub-optimal short-term behaviour. Translated in terms of market behaviour this may imply that e.g. attempts to tie customers or suppliers lead to acceptance of prices (or quantities traded) that are sub-optimal from a partial short-term point of view.

Our general conclusion is that imperfection of the price mechanism is not a purely technical matter, but may have economic causes as well. Whether or not buyers and sellers are willing to accept situations that are sub-optimal from a partial point of view, we believe that it may be worth-while specifying the possibly partial aims underlying their behaviour. Such intentions form the subject matter of the bulk of demand and supply theory, while many of the elements figuring in these theories are suited for statistical observation. It is thus hardly surprising that empirical analysis usually deals with these entities.

However, if adaptation of prices and quantities causes friction, it is not admissable to equate intentions with realisations. In that case a number of intention levels may be specified, dependent on the constraint taken into account. A conventional division is that into <u>ex ante</u> (originally expected or intended), effective (as far as effectuated in demand or supply <u>offers</u> on the market) and actual (realized). Such classifications may be useful, but their content may be somewhat vague if the underlying models are not stated explicitly. The effectiveness of the operational <u>ex ante</u> demand (supply) approach is naturally determined by the possibility of measuring or approximating to this demand (supply). When the approximation is based on ex post realizations, this possibility is in its turn dependent on the possibility of simulating the effects of the adjustment processes stemming from the ex ante divergence of demand and supply. The definition of an ex ante entity is thus a more subjective matter than that of an ex post entity, and the choice of the definition will always depend on the problems to be studied.

Our theoretical labour market model is based on the assumption that (ex ante) intentions may be represented by means of the information available in the period in which the subjects make their economic decisions with regard to intended demand and supply. An additional assumption is that in this period the chances of realising the intentions are uncertain. In theory some type of forecast of these chances might be integrated in the decision process but we will neglect this possibility and assume that the ex ante labour demand is only dependent on wages and labour demand factors, irrespective of the volume of available labour supply.We make analogous assumptions for the ex ante labour supply. The divergence of ex ante demand and ex ante supply generates adaptation processes.

Wages are independent of the current tension on the labour market, but other adjustment mechanisms such as secondary working conditions may diminish the ex ante gap between demand and supply. However, as a rule such adjustments do not clear the market perfectly. The existence of ex post situations conflicting with the desires of the market parties is thus the rule in our model.

The situations we want to cover and our choice of definitions of potential (ex ante) demand for and potential (ex ante) supply of labour are demonstrated by two highly simplified versions of this disequilibrium model for the labour market. The first model (model a) deals with the possibility that non-wage conditions cause some mutual adjustment of demand and supply, the second model (model b) deals with situations in which the adjustment of demand and supply is not based on a common instrument but on (voluntary) internal shifts

within the demanding and supplying households.
Ex post disequilibrium of demand and supply is possible in both models, and it will be demonstrated that both models may be reduced to the same types of functional relationships between actual demand and actual supply on the one hand and potential demand and potential supply on the other hand. These functional relationships are elaborated in chapter 3 and will be applied in the labour market model used for the Netherlands, presented in chapter 6.

Short-run model a assumes rigid wages ($\tilde{p}_1$) and flexible non-wage conditions ($\tilde{n}$).[1] The ratio of the actual value of the non-wage conditions to their 'normal' value ($\tilde{n}_r$) depends on the ratio of potential labour demand to potential labour supply in such a way that the workers get better non-wage conditions if the tension on the labour market increases (eq. 2.5).[2]
Potential or intended labour demand and supply depend not only on prevailing wages, but also on the 'normal' (i.e. not pressure-adjusted) value of the non-wage conditions (eqs. 2.1 and 2.2). This 'normal' value is not dependent on current developments. Both actual labour demand and actual labour supply are partly determined by the actual non-wage conditions (eqs. 2.3 and 2.4). Unemployment is defined both in actual terms (eq. 2.6) and in potential terms (eq. 2.7).
If *ex ante* labour supply exceeds demand the non-price conditions mechanism in this model tends to adjust both supply and demand in such a way that the (*ex post*) difference between actual labour supply and actual labour demand is smaller than the initial difference but not necessarily zero. The same holds *mutatis mutandis* for an *ex ante* excess labour demand situation.

---

1. For symbols and notation we refer to the list of symbols.
2. An example of a relevant non-wage condition is the possibility of part-time work.

Model a

$$\text{Potential demand:} \qquad \tilde{l}_d^p = \tilde{l}_d^p\,(\tilde{p}_1, \tilde{n}_r) \tag{2.1}$$

$$\text{Potential supply:} \qquad \tilde{l}_s^p = \tilde{l}_s^p\,(\tilde{p}_1, \tilde{n}_r) \tag{2.2}$$

$$\text{Actual demand:} \qquad \tilde{l}_d^f = \tilde{l}_d^f\,(\tilde{p}_1, \tilde{n}) \tag{2.3}$$

$$\text{Actual supply:} \qquad \tilde{l}_s^f = \tilde{l}_s^f\,(\tilde{p}_1, \tilde{n}) \tag{2.4}$$

$$\text{Non-wage conditions:} \qquad \tilde{n}/\tilde{n}_r = \tilde{n}/\tilde{n}_r\,(\tilde{l}_d^p/\tilde{l}_s^p) \tag{2.5}$$

$$\text{Actual unemployment:} \qquad \tilde{w}_n^f = \tilde{l}_s^f - \tilde{l}_d^f \tag{2.6}$$

$$\text{Potential unemployment:} \qquad \tilde{w}_n^p = \tilde{l}_s^p - \tilde{l}_d^p \tag{2.7}$$

This model may be reduced to relationships between the ratio of actual labour demand to potential labour demand and the ratio of actual labour supply to potential labour supply on the one hand and the ratio of potential labour demand to potential labour supply on the other hand; assuming proper functional forms we may derive, by substitution of eq. (2.5) and eq. (2.1) into eq. (2.3)

$$\tilde{l}_d^f/\tilde{l}_d^p = \phi_1(\tilde{l}_d^p/\tilde{l}_s^p) \tag{2.8}$$

and similarly by substitution of eqs. (2.5) and (2.2) into eq. (2.4) we arrive at:

$$\tilde{l}_s^f/\tilde{l}_s^p = \phi_2(\tilde{l}_d^p/\tilde{l}_s^p) \tag{2.9}$$

where ϕ_1 and ϕ_2 are functions which will be described later.

Functional relationships like eqs. (2.8) and (2.9) can also be stated directly. This will be done in model b, which does not involve any non-wage condition explicitly. It starts with the assumption that both potential labour demand and potential labour supply depend only on the prevailing rigid wages (eqs. (2.10 and (2.11)). These potential variables should be looked upon as intentions or aims holding for unlimited availibility of labour supply or demand. If, however, limitations do exist, in the sense that e.g. the quantity of labour demanded is not available for the potential buyers at the prevailing wage rate, it may be assumed that the short-term labour demand adjusts itself at least partially through disinvestment in stocks, temporary re-allocation of labour etc. On the other side of the market, short-run excess demand of labour without wage adjustment may lead to adaptation of labour supply by means of participation in the labour force of people not otherwise looking for a job, like married women, pensioners etc.[1] Short-term excess potential labour supply without wage adjustment may cause 'overstaffing'[2] of industries and (temporary) withdrawal from the registered labour force of some of those people who have difficulty in finding a job. In all these situations, disequilibrium exists in the sense that the (ex ante) intentions are not realised.
These types of partial adjustment are formalised in model b.

Model b

Potential demand $\tilde{l}^p_d = \tilde{l}^p_d\ (\tilde{p}_1)$ (2.10)

Potential supply $\tilde{l}^p_s = \tilde{l}^p_s\ (\tilde{p}_1)$ (2.11)

Actual demand $\tilde{l}^f_d/\tilde{l}^p_d = \phi_1^{**}\ (\tilde{l}^p_d/\tilde{l}^p_s)$ (2.12)

Actual supply $\tilde{l}^f_s/\tilde{l}^p_s = \phi_2^{**}\ (\tilde{l}^p_d/\tilde{l}^p_s)$ (2.13)

---

1. This situation is called overemployment by B. Hansen {16}, p. 7.
2. This term was also coined by B. Hansen.

It goes without saying that the assumptions of models a and b may be combined. For the sake of simplicity, we have not done this here. Without discriminating between these two possible approaches, we will assume from now on that relationships like eqs. (2.8) and (2.9) or like eqs. (2.12) and (2.13), or possibly both, apply.

The results of models a and b may be illustrated graphically. For this purpose we assume that the form of the functions ϕ_1 and ϕ_2 (or ϕ_1^{xx} and ϕ_2^{xx}) is such that in the case of coincidence of the intentions of sellors and buyers ($\tilde{l}_d^p = \tilde{l}_s^p$), the actual quantity traded (employment) ($\tilde{l}_d^f$) is equal to both intentions[1] but lower than the actual supply ($\tilde{l}_s^f$).[2]

The actual unemployment may be called 'frictional' unemployment in this situation. We will furthermore assume that the actual unemployment is positive for any wage level. With constant elasticities of potential labour demand and supply with respect to wages the situation is then as sketched in figure 1.

Under the prevailing assumptions, the functions $\tilde{l}_d^p$, $\tilde{l}_s^p$ and $\tilde{l}_d^f$ intersect at one point E. At this point the potential unemployment $\tilde{w}^p_{n_E} = 0$; the actual unemployment $\tilde{w}^f_{n_E}$ is then equal to what we have just called frictional unemployment. As actual unemployment $\tilde{w}_n^f$ is assumed to be always positive, the difference between ln $\tilde{l}_s^f$ and ln $\tilde{l}_d^f$ or $\sim$ ln $(1 + \tilde{w}^f)$ is always positive too.[3] On the other hand,

---

1. In terms of model a this situation is interpretable in that sense that for $\tilde{l}_d^p = \tilde{l}_s^p$ it may be assumed that $\tilde{n} = \tilde{n}_r$; in other words that the non-wage conditions take their 'normal' value for a wage level consistent with equality of potential labour demand and supply
2. As we shall see in chapter 3, the alternative assumption of a lower level of actual employment for a wage level consistent with equality of potential labour demand and supply, as made by Hansen {16} p. 7, does not affect the results of the analysis in first differences (cf. Appendix B).
3. It should be remembered that $\tilde{w}_n$ is the number of unemployed and $\tilde{w}$ is the unemployment expressed as a percentage of labour supply.

potential unemployment $\tilde{w}_n^p$ may become negative, as may $(\ln \tilde{l}_s^p - \ln \tilde{l}_d^p) \sim \ln (1 + \tilde{w}^p)$.

The location of $\tilde{l}_d^f$ with respect to $\tilde{l}_s^p$ and $\tilde{l}_d^p$ may be characterised by a tendency of actual demand to the minimum of potential demand and potential supply. The idea that with rigid prices the lower of these two variables determines sales, since if sales were higher, sellers or buyers would be short, has already been put forward by Frisch {12}.

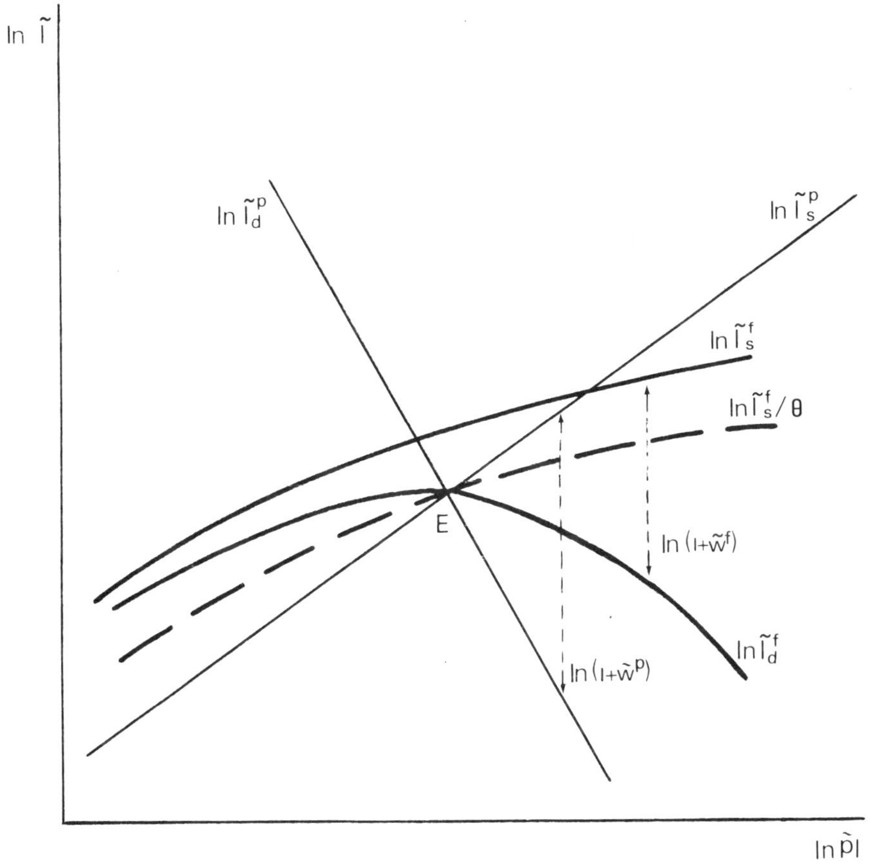

Fig. 1 The Labour Market in Disequilibrium

Theoretically the location of the actual labour supply function $\ln \tilde{l}_s^f$ is more uncertain. In the absence of specific indications to the contrary we will assume that the corrected labour supply curve $(\ln(\tilde{l}_s^f/\theta)$ obtained by diminishing the actual labour supply curve by by a constant fraction $(\frac{\theta-1}{\theta})$ of 'frictional' unemployment always lies between the potential labour supply curve and the potential labour demand curve. This assumption implies that in the case of (positive) ex ante excess labour demand there is, after correction for frictional unemployment, always an adjustment of actual labour supply to potential labour demand, and in the alternative case of (positive) ex ante excess labour supply there is always an adaptation of corrected actual labour supply to potential labour demand. Whether the relative impact of this adjustment increases or decreases if the situation changes from (ex ante) excess labour demand to (ex ante) excess labour supply is difficult to deduce on theoretical grounds. We will assume that this relative impact decreases somewhat, an assumption which is in line with the concavity of the $\ln \tilde{l}_s^f/\theta$ curve towards the origin in figure 1.

3. The estimation method

The principles of the iterative estimation method to be discussed in this chapter are:

1. Actual labour demand and corrected actual labour supply lie between potential labour demand and potential labour supply.
2. The precise location of actual labour demand and corrected actual labour supply between the potential variables is determined by the potential labour demand/supply ratio.
3. Potential labour demand and supply are determined by labour demand theory and labour supply theory respectively.
4. Some potential entities may be represented by their actual counterparts in the initial stages of the computation.
5. These actual values will be gradually replaced by (preliminary) estimates as the iteration proceeds.

The first and the second of these principles represent properties of the actual labour demand and supply functions derived in the preceding chapter. Expression of these properties in mathematical terms follows from discussion of the forms of the functions ϕ_1 and ϕ_2.

In the case of ϕ_1 the location of actual labour demand between potential labour demand and potential labour supply may be expressed mathematically by specifying actual labour demand as a weighted average of potential labour demand and potential labour supply. The second condition is then easily implemented by making the weights

dependent on the potential labour demand/supply ratio.
The function we actually used was suggested to us by Ir. W.J. Keller.
It takes the form:

$$\ln\,(\tilde{i}_d^f/\tilde{i}_d^p) = u_1(\ln\,\tilde{i}_s^p/\tilde{i}_d^p) \tag{3.1.a}$$

or

$$\ln\,\tilde{i}_d^f = u_1\,\ln\,\tilde{i}_s^p + (1-u_1)\,\ln\,\tilde{i}_d^p \tag{3.1.b}$$

where:

$$u_1 = \alpha \tanh(z) + \beta \tag{3.1.c}$$

$$z = \gamma\, x + \ln\,\delta^{\gamma} \tag{3.1.d}$$

$$x = \ln(\tilde{i}_s^p/\tilde{i}_d^p) \tag{3.1.e}$$

and α, β, γ and δ are parameters to be varied.

It is easy to verify that this function may serve our purpose.
Naturally $0 < \tilde{i}_s^p/\tilde{i}_d^p < \infty$,

hence $-\infty < x < \infty$.

If we give γ and δ positive values it follows that

$$-\infty < z < \infty \quad .$$

By definition $\tanh(z) = \dfrac{e^z - e^{-z}}{e^z + e^{-z}}$.

The properties of the hyperbolic tangent are depicted in figure A, Appendix A; it is clear that for

$$-\infty < z < \infty \quad \text{we have} \quad -1 < \tanh(z) < 1 \quad .$$

For u_1 these boundaries imply (according to 3.1.c)

$$-\alpha + \beta < u_1 < \alpha + \beta \quad .$$

Hence the choice of α and β fixes the asymptotes with regard to the position of $\ln \tilde{l}_d^f$ between $\ln \tilde{l}_d^p$ and $\ln \tilde{l}_s^p$ in figure 1. If for instance we want to minimize the weight of potential labour supply (u_1) in the case of extreme (ex ante) excess labour supply ($\tilde{l}_s^p >> \tilde{l}_d^p$) we have:

$\tilde{l}_s^p / \tilde{l}_d^p \to \infty$, so $z \to \infty$ and $\tanh(z) \to +1$ and consequently $u_1 \to \alpha + \beta$.

For a minimum supply weight equal to zero $\alpha + \beta = 0$ or $\alpha = -\beta$.

For a maximum supply weight, on the other hand, we find:

$\tilde{l}_s^p / \tilde{l}_d^p \to 0$, $z \to -\infty$, $\tanh(z) \to -1$ and $u_1 \to -\alpha + \beta$.

Combination of the extreme value $u_1 = 1$ for abundant excess labour demand with $u_1 = 0$ for extreme excess labour demand enables us to compute the proper values for α and β for the equations $\alpha + \beta = 0$ and $-\alpha + \beta = 1$. This yields $\alpha = -0.5$ and $\beta = 0.5$.

The economic interpretation of the asymptotes for the weights in the labour demand equation may be illustrated by a second example that is roughly in line with the parameters ultimately chosen in the estimations. If for any extremely high (positive) value of ex ante excess labour supply at least 10% of this supply surplus is absorbed (in logarithmic terms), $u_1 = \alpha + \beta = 0.10$; if in the opposite situation of extremely high positive values of ex ante excess labour demand at least 40% of this surplus is satisfied, $u_1 = -\alpha + \beta = 0.60$. These two equations can again be solved for α and β. The interpretation of β may be illustrated by putting $\delta = 1$. Equality of potential labour demand and supply ($\tilde{l}_d^p = \tilde{l}_s^p$) then implies $u_1 = \beta$. Hence, β is the equilibrium value of the weight of the potential labour supply in the determination of actual labour demand.[1]

1. The usual assumption that actual transactions are either demand or supply determined may be represented by a choice of parameters that makes u_1 either 1 or 0. Hence, this method contains the conventional hypothesis as a special case. In this respect our approach is more general than alternative attempts to estimate in disequilibrium situations cf. {10}, {15}, {11}, {28}, {14} and {3}.

For further details of the dependence of the weights on the various parameters, we refer to appendix A.

The expression for ϕ_2, the function representing the labour supply, is similar to that for ϕ_1. We have chosen the following form:

$$\ln (\tilde{l}_s^f/\tilde{l}_s^p) = (1 - u_2) \ln (\tilde{l}_d^p/\tilde{l}_s^p) + \ln \theta \qquad (3.2.a)$$

or

$$\ln \tilde{l}_s^f = u_2 \ln \tilde{l}_s^p + (1 - u_2) \ln \tilde{l}_d^p + \ln \theta \qquad (3.2.b)$$

where

$$u_2 = \alpha \tanh(z) + \beta \qquad (3.2.c)$$

$$z = \gamma x + \ln \delta^\gamma \qquad (3.2.d)$$

$$x = \ln (\tilde{l}_s^p/\tilde{l}_d^p) \quad . \qquad (3.2.e)$$

As anticipated in chapter 2 it is assumed 1) that actual labour supply, corrected for a constant fraction $(\frac{\theta-1}{\theta})$ of frictional unemployment, i.e. $\tilde{l}_s^f/\theta$ lies between potential labour demand and potential labour supply and 2) that the weight u_2 of potential labour supply decreases with increasing excess labour supply.[1] The interpretation of the weights in the case of labour supply comes close to that in the case of labour demand. First we have to correct the actual labour supply for frictional unemployment as discussed before. After this operation we may formulate an example (based on the values of α and β ultimately used in the labour supply estimations) in which in the case of abundant excess labour supply at least 25% of the ex ante supply surplus (in logarithmic terms) is withdrawn. Then $1 - u_2 = 0.25$, so $u_2 = 0.75 = \alpha + \beta$; if in the opposite extreme

1. There seems to be some marginal empirical support for the latter assumption; however, the dispersion in the weights ultimately used is so small that the influence of this assumption on the final results is almost negligible.

case at least 15% of the <u>ex ante</u> labour demand surplus is satisfied
(again in logarithmic terms) $1 - u_2 = 0.15$, $u_2 = 0.85 = -\alpha + \beta$.
As before the values of α and β may be computed from these equations.

Some details of the estimation method deserve further elaboration
in this chapter.
For the estimation in terms of relative first differences the
functions (3.1) and (3.2) have to be differentiated with respect to
time.
For eq. (3.1) this gives[1][2]

$$1_d^f = (1 - u_1^x) \, 1_d^p + u_1^x \, 1_s^p \tag{3.3.a}$$

where

$$u_1^x = u_1 + \alpha\gamma\left[1 - \tanh^2(z)\right] \ln \left(\mathring{1}_s^p/\mathring{1}_d^p\right) \tag{3.3.b}$$

The results for eq. (3.2) are similar:

$$1_s^f = (1 - u_2^x) \, 1_d^p + u_2^x \, 1_s^p \tag{3.4.a}$$

where

$$u_2^x = u_2 + \alpha\gamma\left[1 - \tanh^2(z)\right] \ln \left(\mathring{1}_s^p/\mathring{1}_d^p\right) \tag{3.4.b}$$

Now while $0 \leqslant u_1 \leqslant 1$

and $\qquad 0 \leqslant u_2 \leqslant 1$.

the same inequalities do not necessarily hold for u_1^x and u_2^x because
of second-order effects.[2]

In principle eqs. (3.3) and (3.4) may be used as multiplicative
estimation functions for 1_d^f and 1_s^f respectively. However, premulti-

---

1. For notation see the general introduction to the list of symbols.
2. See appendix B.

plication generates linear estimation functions which are easier to handle. In such linear functions the determining factors for l_d^p and l_s^p may be introduced separately, each of them multiplied by the proper weight. Obviously these weights are dependent on the potential labour demand/supply ratio which is not available at the start of the computation. A substitute for this ratio, some index of labour shortage, therefore has to be introduced in the first round of the calculations. The Phillips approach has inspired economists to develop several proxies for this tension on the labour market. For our case we relied on an actual labour supply/demand ratio, derived from the actual unemployment ratio as follows:

$$\tilde{l}_s^f/\tilde{l}_d^f = 1 + \frac{\tilde{w}_f}{100} + \varepsilon$$

where ε represents a correction to the registered unemployment ratio, which centers the scale of the unemployment ratio around a deliberately chosen 'equilibrium level'.[1]

The use of these proxy variables in the first round has a few technical consequences which will be discussed in appendix C. Provisional weights combined with linear terms representing the determining factors for l_d^p and l_s^p enable us to estimate eqs. (3.3) and (3.4). For statistical and technical reasons, however, we made use of actual labour supply in the actual labour demand equation (3.3) and of actual labour demand in the actual labour supply equation (3.4) in the first stage.
The first-round estimations yield a considerable improvement in the information available. Multiplication of the estimated coefficients by the appropriate terms gives a (preliminary) estimate of the changes in potential labour demand and supply. The difference between these growth rates determines the change in the potential

1. If e.g. supply ($\tilde{l}_s^f$) and demand ($\tilde{l}_d^f$) are assumed to be in equilibrium at an unemployment ratio of 2% then ε has to be given the value of -0.02.

unemployment ratio. Accumulation of these changes over time yields a value of this unemployment indicator, which can be used as a basis for a new computation of the weights.
In the second round the provisional ex ante values are introduced everywhere, except that as in the first round l_d^p is represented by its seperate elements in the l_d^f equation and a similar representation is followed for l_s^p in the l_s^f equation. This procedure seems appropriate in view of a possible bias caused by the use of provisional variables in the first round.
The third-round estimation is based on the results of the second round and so on. The iterative procedure generated in this way may converge.[1]

This explanation may have clarified the principles listed as numbers 4 and 5 in the introduction of this chapter. The subject of the third principle, the determination of potential labour demand and supply, will be discussed in the next two chapters.

1. In our experiments it always did. Further research is required to arrive at general conclusions on the properties of the estimation procedure.

4. Potential labour demand

4.1 STATISTICAL INFORMATION AND ANALYTICAL APPROACH

The purpose of this chapter is the derivation of an equation for potential employment in industry. We will start this introduction with a motivation of the approach we have taken, and will continue with a description of the general set-up of this chapter.

From a production point of view it would have been preferable to use other units then people employed, but statistical data about hours actually worked per man for the Netherlands are limited to information about one or two weeks per year for a restricted number of sectors. It therefore seems appropriate to link the conceptual set-up to employment data, which are collected more systematically. Naturally this causes some transformation problems, to which we will return later in this section in the discussion of the contents of section 4.5. First, however, we will state our reasons for the basic choices.

It might be asked why we are trying to estimate potential employment at all, since employment vacancies are registered in the Netherlands. However, the statistical quality of these data as an indication of employers' unfilled demand seems to be questionable. We therefore decided not to use them.

The limitation to employment in industry might also be questioned. There are indications that employment in public administration

is subject to the tensions on the labour market too.[1] Because of the special character of this type of employment, however, this sector was not considered. A disequilibrium analysis of firms' demand for labour would seem to create quite enough complications for the present study!
In our approach, the intended demand for labour follows from the intended supply of products - a fairly conventional assumption. But for each period we distinguish several product-supply levels, each referring to a different ex ante period, related to the possibilities of variation we assume the decision-maker to have.

The first 'supply level' to be considered here is not a supply item from an economic point of view but what might be called the technical production capacity. In section 4.2, the determination of this quantity is worked out on the basis of a clay-clay type production function.
Lagged investments together with technical deterioration determine the technically available stock of capital goods (also simply called machines). Given a constant capital-output coefficient this also determines a technical upper limit to production, which is supposed to be always higher than any conceivable actual supply of products. However, not all vintages present can be used economically. We assume younger vintages to have lower labour requirements. For some

---

1. For our sample period the regression of the yearly changes in government employment on employment in industrial enterprises, the unemployment ratio and a constant yields:

$$100 . \frac{\Delta \tilde{a}_g}{\tilde{a}_{s_{-1}}} = 0.14 \frac{\Delta \tilde{a}_b}{\tilde{a}_{s_{-1}}} . 100 + 0.31 \tilde{w} - 0.37 \qquad \text{var U} \quad R^2 \qquad DW$$

$$(2.8) \qquad (5.1) \qquad (2.8) \qquad 0.022 \quad 0.623 \quad 1.017$$

The positive coefficient of the unemployment rate may be caused by both bottleneck effects and anticyclical employment policy. (For the meaning of the symbols and a description of the statistical characteristics we refer to the list of symbols.)

(older) vintages, marginal (labour) costs may exceed marginal (product) revenue. These vintages are scrapped. Hence, economic obsolescence determines the material (economic) production capacity. With regard to labour demand it is important to note that the resulting age composition of economically usable machinery determines the average labour requirement of capital.
Full (100%) occupation of all these machines gives an output at capacity level. The optimum operating rate under normal conditions may be somewhat lower than 1. In that case, the potential supply of products under normal conditions may be defined as the product of the production capacity and the normal operating rate.
In section 4.2 we determine the labour demand under normal operating rates, on the assumption that all economically usable capital vintages are used in the same proportion in the short run. Hence, the average labour coefficient on all economically usable vintages determines the potential short-term labour demand.
In the next section (4.3) we demonstrate that the derived growth rate of labour demand under normal operating conditions may be split up in three parts:

a) the new employment created by the recent installation of machinery.
b) the loss in employment due to economic obsolescence.
c) the loss in employment due to technical deterioration.

However, in their original form these terms are unsuited for estimation purposes because they contain quite a number of elements which are neither observable nor easily approximated. To get round these problems we apply some modifications on the basis of the properties of the production function and of the assumed equality of marginal labour productivity on the oldest vintage and the corresponding labour renumeration.
These modifications - discussed in sections 4.3.1, 4.3.2 and 4.3.3 - lead in section 4.3.4 to an expression for the growth rate of employment under normal operating conditions with more operational

terms, but which still contains the practically unobservable age of the oldest vintage of capital goods in use. By relating the yearly change in age to the increase in labour productivity from vintage to vintage and the development of real wages, the unknown age may be split up into its (constant) initial value at the beginning of the sample period and the above-mentioned changes. This is done in section 4.3.5.

If only price conditions were relevant, 'normal' (equilibrium) operating rates would be equal to actual operating rates, and equilibrium labour demand would be equal to actual labour demand. But when disequilibrium on the product market is taken into account, non-price conditions may play a role in determining the actual operating rate and hence the actual demand for labour.

In section 4.4.1 we argue that both the growth rate of actual short-term commodity demand and the initial utilisation rate of material production capacity may contribute to the approximation to the intended short-term supply of commodities. In this way, disequilibrium on the product market has an explicit impact on demand in the labour market.[1]

It is widely recognized that disequilibrium may govern the financial markets. As a possible spill-over effect on the labour market the change in business-liquidity position is introduced as an additional determinant of labour demand in section 4.4.2.

Section 4.5 deals with the problems caused by the changes in hours worked per man. For the transformation of labour demand in terms of labour units consisting of a constant number of working hours per man per year into labour demand in terms of number of men employed, we divide changes in hours worked per man into:

a) structural changes - changes in contractual working time.
b) short-term changes, deviations from contractual hours caused by overtime, illness, strikes etc.

---

1. Cf. Patinkin {30}, chapter XIII.

For the last type of changes we assume domination of the cyclical elements and hence introduce a simple implicit demand function for overtime. This matter is discussed in 4.5.2.
For the contractual working hours, we use an approximative index for workers employed in industrial enterprises, and assume that changes in this index lead to changes in the demand for labour (in terms of men employed) which are inversely proportional to the changes in the index itself. This assumption is elaborated in 4.5.1.
A change in working time will generally affect the machine operating time. For our purposes, we assume the machine hours to be proportional to contractual working hours. The consequences of this relation are studied in 4.5.3.
Another impact of change in hours worked is the inadequacy of labour renumeration per man as an index for labour cost per unit time. Appropriate corrections are elaborated in section 4.5.4.
Finally, all the elements of the potential labour demand are combined in section 4.6.

4.2 THE PRODUCTION FUNCTION AND DERIVED DEMAND FOR LABOUR UNDER NORMAL OPERATING CONDITIONS

This section deals with the technical relations between production, labour demand and investment. The whole analysis in this section runs in terms of firms' intentions under normal operating conditions. The clay-clay type production model that will be used disaggregates the capital goods into (yearly) vintages.[1] Its main characteristics are:

a) There are two production factors, labour and capital, producing one type of commodity.

1. For relevant literature see Baum et al. {5}, Solow et al. {35}, Isard {19}, De Vries {40}, Allen {2} , Den Hartog and Tjan {17}.

b) Labour is homogeneous. Its units in this stage of the analysis[1] are workers with a constant number of working hours per year. Capital consists of units, labeled machines, varying from vintage to vintage. The vintages are denoted by τ, $\tau = t$, $t-1$, $t-2$, ... etc. In line with the assumption concerning the working hours of labour the operating time of machines per year is constant.[1]

c) For each vintage, labour and capital are complementary production factors. Machines from vintage τ require a constant number of workers κ_τ during their whole lifetime to produce one unit of output. The capital required to produce one unit of output (capital coefficient) ν is equal for all vintages ($\nu_\tau = \nu_{\tau-1} = ... = \nu$), but the labour coefficient - the number of workers required to produce one unit of output - increases with the age of the capital vintages. The growth of labour productivity from vintage to vintage is caused by the improvement in the quality of the machinery; in other words, technical progress is capital-embodied. The growth rate of labour productivity from vintage τ to vintage $\tau+1$ is equal to η for any τ. Hence

$$\frac{1}{\kappa_\tau} = \frac{1}{\kappa_{\tau-1}} (1 + \eta') \quad \text{for } \tau = t, t-1, t-2 \text{ ... etc.} \qquad (4.2.1)$$

where $\eta' = 0.01\eta$.

d) As mentioned above this whole chapter deals with firms' intentions. With respect to the potential supply of commodities, two aspiration levels are relevant in this context. The first is the 'normal' potential supply, which is a constant fraction ('normal' operating rate) of the economic production capacity. The economic production capacity is that part of the technical production capacity whose use is profitable from the point of

1. We will modify this assumption later.

view of a comparison of marginal cost and marginal revenue on the basis of relative prices. The technical production capacity is the total output of all capital goods (machinery) irrespective of the profitability. The latter output is assumed to be always higher than any conceivable effective supply of commodities.

The second aspiration level might be called the effective (short-term) potential supply. The discussion of the consequences of the fact that it is more realistic to assume that firms basically do not operate under something like normal conditions, and adapt their short-term intended operating rate to the instantaneous demand/supply conditions will be postponed to section 4.4.1. In the present section, only 'normal' conditions will be considered.

e) Excess capacity as assumed under d) leads to some idle machinery.
f) The gestation period for machinery is one year.
g) The technical deterioration of machinery takes place according to a fixed percentage ρ per year and starts in the second year of use.

Some conclusions may be drawn from the foregoing properties and assumptions. For a given production target or, which comes to the same thing, for a given potential supply of commodities the distribution of manpower over machinery determines the labour requirements. Cost minimizing will lead to priority for the newest machines, which require the lowest labour input. The next candidates for employment are the machines that are one year older, and so on till the target production volume is attained. The remaining machines stay idle. Allen indicates these capital goods as 'machines stored in mothballs'.[1]

On the basis of the assumptions just mentioned, we can study the relations between potential output, employment and investment

1. R.G.D. Allen {2} p. 300.

for capital goods of vintage τ.
If we represent the investment in period τ by i_τ, the available capital goods of this vintage in period t, $i_{\tau,t}$, are given:

$$\tilde{i}_{\tau,t} = (1 - \rho')^{t-1-\tau}\tilde{i}_\tau$$

where $\rho' = 0.01\rho$.

We now denote the technically possible output of this vintage by $\tilde{y}_{s_{\tau,t}}$ and the number of workers required to operate the vintage by $\tilde{l}_{\tau,t}$. The production function for vintage τ in period t may then be written as:

$$\tilde{y}_{s_{\tau,t}} = \frac{(1 - \rho')^{t-1-\tau}\tilde{i}_\tau}{\nu} = \frac{\tilde{l}_{\tau,t}}{\kappa_\tau} \qquad (4.2.2)$$

where τ = t-1, t-2 ... etc.

For capital goods from an individual vintage we may conclude that technical deterioration causes production and employment of machinery to fall by ρ% per year. Of course, scrapping because of economic obsolescence reduces production and employment of a given vintage to zero.
For our purpose we are interested in employment on all vintages in use in a certain year t.
Let $\tilde{m}_t$ be the age of the oldest vintage used in year t.
Then:

$$\tilde{y}_{s_{\tau,t}} > 0 \text{ and } \tilde{l}_{\tau,t} > 0 \quad \text{if } \tau = t-1, t-2 \ldots\ldots, t-\tilde{m}_t$$

To find $\tilde{y}_{s_t}$, the total potential production in year t, we must sum the potential production volumes of the individual vintages in year t:

$$\tilde{y}_{s_t} = \sum_{\tau=t-1}^{t-\tilde{m}_t} \tilde{y}_{s_{\tau,t}} = \frac{1}{\nu} \sum_{\tau=t-1}^{t-\tilde{m}_t} (1 - \rho')^{t-1-\tau} \tilde{i}_\tau = \frac{1}{\nu} \tilde{k}_t \qquad (4.2.3)$$

where $\tilde{k}_t$ represents the capital stock required to produce the total potential production volume in year t under normal operating conditions.

For the corresponding total potential employment $\tilde{l}_t$ in year t under normal operating conditions we obtain:

$$\tilde{l}_t = \sum_{\tau=t-1}^{t-\tilde{m}_t} \tilde{l}_{\tau,t} = \frac{1}{\nu} \sum_{\tau=t-1}^{t-\tilde{m}_t} \kappa_\tau (1 - \rho')^{t-1-\tau} \tilde{i}_\tau \qquad (4.2.4)$$

From eq. (4.2.4) we derive the following expression for the yearly absolute change in potential employment under normal operating conditions:

$$\tilde{l}_t - \tilde{l}_{t-1} = \frac{\kappa_{t-1} \tilde{i}_{t-1}}{\nu} - \frac{1}{\nu} \sum_{\tau=t-1=t-\tilde{m}_t}^{t-1-\tilde{m}_{t-1}} \kappa_\tau (1 - \rho')^{t-2-\tau} \tilde{i}_\tau -$$

$$- \frac{1}{\nu} \sum_{\tau=t-2}^{t-\tilde{m}_t} \kappa_\tau \left[(1 - \rho')^{t-2-\tau} - (1 - \rho')^{t-1-\tau} \right] \tilde{i}_\tau \qquad (4.2.5)$$

The first term on the right-hand side may be interpreted as the change in potential employment caused merely by the newly installed vintage, the second term stands for the loss in potential employment due to economic obsolescence of machinery and the third term for the loss in potential employment caused by technical deterioration of machinery.

To facilitate the discussion of these three elements in the next sections, eq. (4.2.5) will be rewritten. Firstly, the loss in potential employment due to economic obsolescence can be defined as:

$$\Delta \tilde{le}_t = \frac{1}{\nu} \sum_{\tau=t-1-\tilde{m}_t}^{t-1-\tilde{m}_{t-1}} \kappa_\tau (1-\rho')^{t-2-\tau} \tilde{i}_\tau \qquad (4.2.6)$$

Secondly the last term on the right-hand side of eq. (4.2.5) can be rearranged. We then obtain:

$$\tilde{l}_t - \tilde{l}_{t-1} = \frac{\kappa_{t-1}\, i_{t-1}}{\nu} - \Delta \tilde{le}_t - \frac{\rho'}{\nu} \sum_{\tau=t-2}^{t-\tilde{m}_t} \kappa_\tau (1-\rho')^{t-2-\tau} \tilde{i}_\tau \qquad (4.2.7)$$

Or in terms of percentage changes:

$$l_t = 100\, \frac{\tilde{l}_t - \tilde{l}_{t-1}}{\tilde{l}_{t-1}} = 100\, \frac{\kappa_{t-1}\, \tilde{i}_{t-1}}{\nu \tilde{l}_{t-1}} - 100\, \frac{\Delta \tilde{le}_t}{\tilde{l}_{t-1}} -$$

$$- \frac{\rho}{\nu \tilde{l}_{t-1}} \sum_{\tau=t-2}^{t-\tilde{m}_t} (1-\rho')^{t-2-\tau} \tilde{i}_\tau \qquad (4.2.8)$$

4.3 THE THREE ELEMENTS OF POTENTIAL EMPLOYMENT

4.3.1 Potential employment on the newest vintage

To start the discussion on the elements of eq. (4.2.5) or eq. (4.2.8) we will turn to the first term on the right-hand side.
Labour productivity on the newest, i.e. the most recently installed, vintage may be expressed in terms of that on the oldest vintage in use in the following way (cf. eq. (4.2.1)).

$$\kappa_{t-1} = \kappa_{t-1-\tilde{m}_{t-1}} (1 + \eta')^{-\tilde{m}_{t-1}} \qquad (4.3.1)$$

A vintage will be kept in use as long as its production value is equal to or greater than the variable labour costs incurred. Given the assumed technical progress this implies that labour productivity on the oldest vintage in use equals the real wage rate

$$\kappa_{t-1-\tilde{m}_{t-1}} = (\tilde{p}_y/\tilde{p}_1)_{t-1} \qquad (4.3.2)$$

where $\tilde{p}_1$: wage rate per labour unit as previously determined

$\tilde{p}_y$: price of production.

Substitution of eq. (4.3.2) into eq. (4.3.1) yields:

$$\kappa_{t-1} = (\tilde{p}_y/\tilde{p}_1)_{t-1} (1 + \eta')^{-\tilde{m}_{t-1}} \qquad (4.3.3)$$

Defining labours' share of the total income $\tilde{F}_t$ as

$$\tilde{F}_t = \frac{\tilde{p}_{1_t} \tilde{l}_t}{\tilde{p}_{y_t} \tilde{y}_{s_t}} \qquad (4.3.4)$$

we can use eqs. (4.3.3) and (4.3.4) to modify the first term on the right-hand side of eq. (4.2.8) to:

$$100. \frac{\kappa_{t-1} \tilde{i}_{t-1}}{\nu \tilde{l}_{t-1}} = \frac{100}{\nu \tilde{F}_{t-1}} \frac{\tilde{i}_{t-1}}{\tilde{y}_{s_{t-1}}} (1 + \eta')^{-\tilde{m}_{t-1}} \qquad (4.3.5)$$

4.3.2 The loss in potential employment caused by economic obsolescence

In section 4.2 we denoted the loss in potential employment due to economic obsolescence by $\Delta \tilde{le}_t$. We now denote the corresponding loss in potential production by $\Delta \tilde{y}_{se_t}$ and the average labour productivity on machinery becoming obsolete in year t by $(\kappa_{e_t})^{-1}$. Then by definition we arrive at the following expression:

$$\Delta \tilde{le}_t = \Delta \tilde{y}_{se_t} \kappa_{e_t} \tag{4.3.6}$$

If the number of vintages to be scrapped due to economic obsolescence comes close to one and monopolistic forces do not upset competitive labour renumeration appreciably, one year lagged real wages may be used as an approximation to the average labour productivity on obsolete machinery. Hence:

$$(\kappa_{e_t})^{-1} = (\tilde{p}_1/\tilde{p}_y)_{t-1} \tag{4.3.7}$$

The other unspecified element in eq. (4.3.6), $\Delta \tilde{y}_{se_t}$ can be derived by differentiating $\tilde{y}_{s_t}$ in the same way as was done with $\tilde{l}_t$.
From eq. (4.2.3) we obtain:

$$\tilde{y}_{s_t} - \tilde{y}_{s_{t-1}} = \frac{1}{\nu} \tilde{i}_{t-1} - \frac{1}{\nu} \sum_{\tau=t-1-\tilde{m}_t}^{t-1-\tilde{m}_{t-1}} (1 - \rho')^{t-2-\tau} \tilde{i}_\tau -$$

$$- \frac{\rho'}{\nu} \sum_{\tau=t-2}^{t-\tilde{m}_t} (1 - \rho')^{t-2-\tau} \tilde{i}_\tau \tag{4.3.8}$$

Defining $\Delta\tilde{y}_{se_t} = \frac{1}{\nu} \sum_{\tau=t-1-\tilde{m}_t}^{t-1-\tilde{m}_{t-1}} (1 - \rho')^{t-2-\tau} \tilde{i}_\tau$ and rearranging the last term, we can reduce eq. (4.3.8) to:

$$\tilde{y}_{s_t} - \tilde{y}_{s_{t-1}} = \frac{1}{\nu} \tilde{i}_{t-1} - \Delta\tilde{y}_{se_t} - \rho'\tilde{y}_{s_{t-1}} + \frac{\rho'}{\nu} \sum_{\tau=t-1-\tilde{m}_t}^{t-1-\tilde{m}_{t-1}} (1 - \rho')^{t-2-\tau} \tilde{i}_\tau \tag{4.3.9}$$

Neglecting the relatively small last term on the right-hand side of eq. (4.3.9) and dividing by $\tilde{y}_{s_{t-1}}$, we find:

$$y_{s_t} = 100 \frac{\tilde{y}_{s_t} - \tilde{y}_{s_{t-1}}}{\tilde{y}_{s_{t-1}}} = \frac{100}{\nu} \frac{\tilde{i}_{t-1}}{\tilde{y}_{s_{t-1}}} - 100 \frac{\Delta\tilde{y}_{se_t}}{\tilde{y}_{s_{t-1}}} - \rho \tag{4.3.10}$$

Now we are able to rewrite the second term on the right-hand side of eq. (4.2.8). According to eqs. (4.3.6), (4.3.7), (4.3.10) and (4.3.4) we have:

$$- 100 \frac{\Delta\tilde{l}_{e_t}}{\tilde{l}_{t-1}} = - \frac{1}{\tilde{F}_{t-1}} \left[- y_{s_t} + \frac{100}{\nu} \frac{\tilde{i}_{t-1}}{\tilde{y}_{s_{t-1}}} - \rho \right] \tag{4.3.11}$$

Eq. (4.3.11) will be used as an <u>indirect</u> representation of the relative change in potential employment due to economic obsolescence.

4.3.3 The loss in potential employment caused by technical deterioration

The last term on the right-hand side of eq. (4.2.8) can be treated in the following way:

$$- \frac{\rho}{\nu \tilde{l}_{t-1}} \sum_{\tau=t-2}^{t-\tilde{m}_t} \kappa_\tau (1-\rho')^{t-2-\tau} \tilde{i}_\tau =$$

$$= - \rho + \frac{\rho}{\nu \tilde{l}_{t-1}} \sum_{\tau=t-1-\tilde{m}_t}^{t-1-\tilde{m}_{t-1}} \kappa_\tau (1-\rho)^{t-2-\tau} \tilde{i}_\tau \qquad (4.3.12)$$

In this expression the last term on the right-hand side is relatively small and can be neglected. The loss in potential employment due to technical deterioration is thus approximately equal to ρ.

4.3.4 Combination of the three elements

The elements discussed in this section can now be combined. Substitution of eqs. (4.3.5), (4.3.11) and (4.3.12) into eq. (4.2.8) yields:

$$l_t = \frac{100}{\nu \tilde{F}_{t-1}} \frac{\tilde{i}_{t-1}}{\tilde{y}_{s_{t-1}}} (1+\eta')^{-\tilde{m}_{t-1}} - \frac{1}{\tilde{F}_{t-1}} \left[- y_{s_t} + \frac{100}{\nu} \frac{\tilde{i}_{t-1}}{\tilde{y}_{s_{t-1}}} - \rho \right] - \rho$$

(4.3.13)[1]

The terms on the right-hand side are respectively:

---

1. Some terms of eq. (4.3.13) have to be combined for estimation purposes. This will be done in chapter 6.

- The contribution of employment on the newest vintage as a function of the lagged investment ratio, the lagged share of labour in the total income, the growth rate of productivity per vintage and the age of the oldest vintage.
- The loss in potential employment caused by economic obsolescence of machinery as a function of labour's share of the income, the growth rate of the intended product supply, the investment ratio and the rate of technical deterioration.
- The loss in potential employment caused by the constant rate of technical deterioration of machinery.

Eq. (4.3.13) refers to employment under 'normal' operating conditions. It still lacks several possible impacts on employment mentioned in the introduction. Before we come to these refinements, however, we will consider the representation of the age of the oldest vintage in use ($\tilde{m}_{t-1}$).

4.3.5 The age of the oldest vintage in use

Eq. (4.3.13) contains $\tilde{m}_{t-1}$, the age of the oldest vintage one year ago, an entity for which no reliable statistical information is available. To circumvent this problem we will approximate $\tilde{m}_{t-1}$ by:

$$\tilde{m}_{t-1} = \tilde{m}_o + \sum_{t=1}^{t-1} \Delta\tilde{m}_t \qquad (4.3.14)$$

where $\tilde{m}_o$ is a deliberately chosen value of the age of the oldest vintage in a base year, and $\Delta\tilde{m}_t$ stands for the yearly change in this age in absolute terms. This change in its turn can be approximately derived from the development of real wages. That this is so may be demonstrated in the following way. Using eq. (4.3.3) with respect to year t we get:

$$\kappa_t = (\tilde{p}_y/\tilde{p}_l)_t \, (1 + \eta')^{-\tilde{m}_t} \qquad (4.3.15)$$

Taking natural logarithms and differentiating with respect to time yields:

$$100 \frac{\Delta\kappa_t}{\kappa_{t-1}} = (p_y - p_1)_t - 100 \ln (1 + \eta')\Delta\tilde{m}_t \tag{4.3.16}$$

According to eq. (4.2.1) $100 \frac{\Delta\kappa_t}{\kappa_{t-1}} = - \eta$ (4.3.17)

hence $- \eta = (p_y - p_1)_t - 100 \ln (1 + \eta')\Delta\tilde{m}_t$ (4.3.18)

and $\Delta\tilde{m}_t = \frac{\eta + (p_y - p_1)_t}{100 \ln (1+\eta')}$ (4.3.19)

Substitution into eq. (4.3.14) yields:

$$\tilde{m}_{t-1} = \tilde{m}_o + \sum_{t=1}^{t-1} \frac{\eta - (p_1 - p_y)_t}{100 \ln (1+\eta')} \tag{4.3.20}$$

In this way we have derived an indirect way of representing the age of the oldest vintage figuring in eq. (4.3.13). The representation of another variable of eq. (4.3.13), the potential product supply y_{s_t}, will be discussed in the next section.

4.4 THE EFFECTS OF DISEQUILIBRIUM ON OTHER MARKETS

Since Patinkin {30} and Clower {8}, a possible spill-over of a disequilibrium on one market to other markets is accepted as a theoretical possibility. However, the theoretical discussion initiated by these authors has hardly led to any serious elaboration of their ideas adapted to the requirements for empirical implementation. On the other hand examples of elements in empirical studies that are interpretable as indicators of disequilibria on other markets are not difficult to find. In the present publication we will not try to fill this gap, because in our view this requires a special study. Anticipating the results we expect from such an investigation we will assume that disequilibria on the product market as well as on financial markets will have an impact on the demand for labour.

4.4.1 Intended short-term supply of commodities

If firms could always produce at normal operating rates, the potential labour demand as derived in section 4.3 would always be equal to the effective labour demand. The growth rates of actual production would then always be equal to that of the production capacity; however, there are several indications that firms' operating rates tend to fluctuate considerably. Apparently, the price mechanism is not so flexible as to lead to equality of demand and supply for any period.
Economic adaptation processes generally cost time and money; and the more drastic the changes are, the higher the costs involved. On the basis of these considerations we distinguish several decision levels with regard to the supply of products. In this analysis the investment decision which results in the determination of the technical limits to product supply is predetermined. The problem of scrapping, leading to the fixation of the economic production capacity, was discussed in section 4.3 as a partial optimalisation problem dependent on relative prices. This section deals with the determination of the volume of intended short-term product supply, or the choice of the short-term operating rate. In this context we assume that in the short term, price adaptation leading to stabilisation of the operating rate at the normal level is impossible. Nevertheless, if we assume that this normal level is the optimum one, firms have an incentive to meet an increase in demand by eliminating an initial difference between the actual operating rate and the normal one. This is the reason why we assume that the growth

rate of the intended short-term supply of commodities depends not only on the expected short-term demand, but also on the initial difference between potential demand and potential ('long-term') supply of products. Before we formalize this dependence, we have to explain the notation that we will adopt.
As stated above, the analysis of chapter 4 is generally in terms of intentions or expectations. So far, in the case of ex ante variables we only indicated the reference period: the period for which the anticipation holds. When it comes to representation of ex ante variables by means of ex post entities a more precise dating is required. In the following argument we will consider both the reference period - the period for which the decisions are made, indicated by the first subindex t - and the period in which the anticipations that lead to decisions with regard to the reference period are made - indicated by the second sub-index t^x. In this notation l_{t,t^x} stands for the (planned) demand for labour in period t, as anticipated in period t^x.
In this notation the relation between intended short-term supply of products, expected demand and initial excess supply may be expressed as follows:

$$y_{sc_{t,t^x}} = y_{d_{t,t^x}} - \theta_1 \left[\frac{\tilde{y}_{sn_{t^x}} - \tilde{y}_{d_{t^x}}}{\tilde{y}_{sn_{t^x}}} \right] . 100 \qquad (4.4.1)$$

where:

$y_{sc_{t,t^x}}$ the growth rate of the current supply of products in period t, as anticipated in period t^x.

$y_{d_{t,t^x}}$ the expected growth rate of demand for products.

$\tilde{y}_{sn_{t^x}}$ the 'normal' product supply level in the decision period t^x (potential supply based on a normal operating rate).

$\tilde{y}_{d_{t^x}}$ the level of potential demand for products in the decision period t^x.

It should be noted that according to eq. (4.4.1) supply follows demand if the operating rate is optimum in the initial period. Hence an accurate forecast of demand in this case implies maintenance of this optimum operating rate (if, of course, no error is made in the forecast of potential product supply). In the case of a non-optimum operating rate in the initial period, a fraction θ_1 of the initial excess product supply is eliminated in the reference period.

Next, we assume that the growth rate of the expected demand for products may be approximated to by the actual demand and a trend term in the following way:

$$y_{d_{t,t^{*}}} = \theta_2 \, y^{*}_{d_t} + (1 - \theta_2)\theta_3 \qquad (4.4.2)$$

where:

$y^{*}_{d_t}$ is the growth rate of the actual demand for products

and

θ_3 might be interpreted as the normally expected value of this growth rate.

It seems inadequate to equate $y^{*}_{d_t}$ to the actual growth rate of production of firms in period t since one of its elements, short-term agricultural production, is highly supply-determined. We therefore correct for harvest fluctuations by means of the expression:

$$y^{*}_{d_t} = y_{d_t} - \theta_4 \, y_{1a_t} \qquad (4.4.3)$$

where:

y_d is the actual growth rate of production of firms and

y_{1a} stands for the difference between the actual growth rate of agricultural production and its average trend rate of growth.

We now approximate to the potential relative excess product supply by a measure of the <u>ex post</u> excess production capacity. For this purpose, we define:

$$\tilde{s}_{t^x} \equiv \frac{\tilde{y}_{d_t x} - \tilde{y}_{sn_t x}}{\tilde{y}_{sn_t x}} \cdot 100 \qquad (4.4.4)$$

and assume:

$$\tilde{s}_{t^x} = - \theta_5 \, \tilde{q}_{t-1} \qquad (4.4.5)$$

Where $\tilde{q}$ is an index of relative excess production capacity, expressed as a deviation from its average value during the sample period.[1]

We can now combine all the elements of the approximate growth rate of the current potential supply of products.

Substitution of eqs. (4.4.2), (4.4.3), (4.4.4) and (4.4.5) into eq. (4.4.1) gives:

$$y_{sc_{t,t^x}} = \theta_2(y_{d_t} - \theta_4 y_{1a_t}) + (1 - \theta_2)\theta_3 - \theta_1\theta_5 \, \tilde{q}_{t-1} \qquad (4.4.6)$$

This expression for the growth rate of the current potential supply of products will be substituted into eq. (4.3.13) in section 4.6. The latter equation also involves the level of the potential supply of products. Because of the minor numerical importance of such corrections on level variables we neglect any possible impact of a replacement of normal supply levels by actual supply levels in this equation.

4.4.2 Business liquidity position

There are several reasons why disequilibrium on financial markets

---

1. The value of $\tilde{s}$ is 0 for markets in equilibrium, hence it seems appropriate to scale $\tilde{q}$ around an average value.

could have an impact on the labour market. Perhaps the most simple reason is the fact that wages have to be financed.[1] Any change in firms' capacity to do so may have an impact on the volume of their demand for labour. Another, more sophisticated transmission channel may be labelled the 'monetary impact on the business climate'. Here we touch upon the discussion between 'Monetarists' and 'Keynesians'. It is hardly our purpose to add to this dispute in the context of this study. As a global indication of the possible operational consequences of our opinion we may point out the possibility that <u>ex ante</u> tension on the product market is poorly reflected in <u>ex post</u> operating rates. Indicators of tension on financial markets may add part of the omitted information in this respect.[2]
In view of the difficulties involved in the development of expressions dealing more adequately with the different ways in which financial situations affect labour demand, we will confine ourselves to a very simple relationship between the potential labour demand of enterprises and their business liquidity position, of the following type:

$$\tilde{l}_{b_t} = \mu_o \, \tilde{l}_t \, \tilde{l}_{q_t}^{\mu} \tag{4.4.7}$$

where:

$\tilde{l}_t$: potential labour demand as previously determined, excluding monetary influences

$\tilde{l}_{b_t}$: potential labour demand, including monetary influences

---

1. Cf. Verdoorn et al. {39}.
2. More adequate, but too complicated to incorporate in the present analysis would seem to be a three-market disequilibrium analysis. For a theoretical discussion we may refer to Clower {8} in this context, as for the empirical approach the generalisation of our method to three markets seems applicable. An empirical basis for the analysis of the monetary sector of the Dutch economy is to be found in A. Knoester {22} and P.D. van Loo {26}. For an interesting attempt to link the monetary sector to the real sector cf. A. Knoester and P. Buitelaar {23}.

$\tilde{l}_{q_t}$: anticipated liquidity ratio of industries, approximated by dividing time deposits + demand deposits + call money + savings deposits at commercial banks + foreign-currency deposits, all held by the public, by the value of production of industries

Taking natural logarithms and differentiating with respect to time, we find:

$$l_{b_t} = l_t + \mu l_{q_t} \tag{4.4.8}$$

4.5 CHANGES IN WORKING HOURS

4.5.1 General approach and direct impact of variations in contractual working hours

As anticipated in the introduction to this chapter the development of equations for estimation of the potential labour demand in terms of men employed is complicated by the fact that the actual variation of working hours in the sample period is poorly reflected in the available statistical information. This situation forced us to neglect the scattered data about hours actually worked and to rely only on an approximative index of contractual working time for workers employed in all enterprises. As an analytical counterpart of this dichotomy in the data we distinguish between two types of variation in the potential number of hours worked per man per year:

a) the changes in contractual working time ('structural' changes) ($\tilde{h}_c$)
b) other variations, deviations from contractual hours caused by overtime, illness, strikes etc. ($\tilde{o}_b$).

These potential entities are linked to potential labour demand in terms of a constant number of working hours ($\tilde{l}_b$) and to potential labour demand in terms of men employed ($\tilde{a}_b$) by means of the following definition:

$$\tilde{l}_{b_t} = \tilde{a}_{b_t} \, \tilde{h}_{c_t} \, \tilde{o}_{b_t} \qquad (4.5.1)$$

We neglect any possible direct influence of changes in working hours on the labour productivity per hour. Hence, we assume the volume of men employed to be inversely proportional to the change in working hours, at least in this section.[1]
Differentiating eq. (4.5.1) with respect to time and rearranging terms, we obtain an expression for the growth rate of labour demand in terms of potential employment expressed in man-years:

$$a_{b_t} = l_{b_t} - h_{c_t} - o_{b_t} \qquad (4.5.2)$$

The representation of the first two elements of the right-hand side of eq. (4.5.2), l_{b_t} and h_{c_t}, offers no special problems. For l_{b_t} labour demand in man-hours, we refer to the formulas developed earlier in this chapter; for h_{c_t}, contractual working time, we use direct statistical information. However, the short-term variations in working time o_{b_t} require a special treatment. This will be done in the next section. Other problems caused by changes in working hours will be dealt with in sections 4.5.3 and 4.5.4. In section 4.5.3 we link machine operating time to contractual working hours, and in section 4.5.4 we transform the labour renumeration per man employed into labour costs per unit work time.

4.5.2 Overtime variations

As stated in the preceding section, short-term fluctuations in

1. In the next section we will study possible cyclic fluctuations caused by overtime.

working time may have several causes. We mentioned overtime, illness and strikes. There is some statistical information about losses in labour time due to illness, strikes and bad weather, but for simplicity we assume that overtime is the dominant cause of changes in short-term deviations from contractual working time. The theory of overtime is not far developed. For our purposes, we assume the demand for overtime to increase in periods in which the growth of potential labour demand is relatively high and in periods in which the cut in contractual working hours is above average. This This leads to the following relation:

$$o_{b_t} = \zeta_1(l_{b_t} - \overline{l_{b_t}}) - \zeta_2(h_{c_t} - \overline{h_{c_t}}) \tag{4.5.3}$$

where $\overline{l_{b_t}}$ represents the average growth rate of potential labour demand (in man-hours per year) during some 'normal' period, for which we take the sample period, while $\overline{h_{c_t}}$ symbolizes the average growth rate of potential contractual working hours during the same period. Both parameters ζ_1 and ζ_2 are by definition positive.
Eq. (4.5.3) implies that in the short run 1% surplus in the growth rate of potential labour demand l_{b_t} over its average value $\overline{l_{b_t}}$ is compensated for by an increase in overtime o_{b_t} of ζ_1(%).
Similarly a 1% more than average decrease in contractual working hours causes a rise in (short-run) overtime by ζ_2(%).
Although simple, the above expression may suffice for our purposes.

4.5.3 The change in real wages per unit labour time

As mentioned above, the approximate expression for the labour costs is affected by changes in working time. The percentage change in real wages $(p_1 - p_y)$ on which eq. (4.3.20) is based contains the value-added price of a worker defined in the beginning of section 4.2 as a labour unit consisting of a constant number of working hours per year. In order to compute the adequate relative wage rate in the case of a changing number of working hours per man, the actual average wage rate per man ($\tilde{p}_{1b}$) with a varying number of working hours should be corrected for the average working time in the following way:

$$\tilde{p}_1 = \tilde{p}_{1b}/\tilde{h}_c \quad (4.5.4)$$

[1]

or in percentage rates of change (taking natural logarithms and differentiating with respect to time):

$$p_1 = p_{1b} - h_c \quad (4.5.5)$$

4.5.4 Impact of contractual working hours on machine operating time

So far, we explicitly neglected any change in operating hours of machinery. Actually, the contractual working hours for labour fell considerably in our sample period. In the absence of any specific information we assume an equal change in machine operating time.[2] This assumption may be incorporated in the analysis by multiplying the volume of investments by the appropriate operating time index in eq. (4.3.13) or, which amounts to the same thing, by substituting into (4.3.13):

---

1. The use of contractual working time instead of actual working time seems appropriate in this case, because of the cyclic character of overtime and in view of the fact that it is the average renumeration over some years that counts in this respect rather than the outcome for one specific year. The latter consideration will lead us to some smoothing of real wages, as discussed in section 4.6.
2. Actually there are arguments for both a more than equal and a less than equal change: in general, shorter working time will cause a less efficient use of capital goods, but for some sectors introduction of shifts led to a more intensive use of capital goods.

$$\nu_t = \nu_o / \tilde{h}_{c_t} \qquad (4.5.6)$$

where ν_o represents the capital coefficient in the base year and $\tilde{h}_{c_t}$ the contractual working-hours index in year t.

4.6 THE FINAL EXPRESSION

At this stage of the analysis the separate elements of potential labour demand developed earlier in this chapter will be combined. Our starting point is eq. (4.5.2). Substitution of eqs. (4.5.3), (4.4.8), (4.3.13) and (4.5.6) gives:

$$a_{b_t} = \frac{100}{\nu_o \tilde{F}_{t-1}} (1 - \zeta_1)\, \tilde{h}_{c_t}\, (\tilde{i}/\tilde{y}_s)_{t-1}\, (1 + \eta')^{-\tilde{m}_{t-1}} +$$

$$+ \frac{(1 - \zeta_1)\, y_{s_t}}{\tilde{F}_{t-1}} - \frac{100(1 - \zeta_1)}{\nu_o \tilde{F}_{t-1}} \tilde{h}_{c_t}\, (\tilde{i}/\tilde{y}_s)_{t-1} + \frac{(1 - \zeta_1)\rho}{\tilde{F}_{t-1}} -$$

$$- (1 - \zeta_1)\rho + (1 - \zeta_1)\mu\, l_{q_t} - (1 - \zeta_2)\, h_{c_t} + \zeta_1 \overline{l_{b_t}} - \zeta_2 \overline{h_{c_t}}$$

(4.6.1)

Furthermore eq. (4.5.5) can be substituted into eq. (4.3.20), which yields:

$$\tilde{m}_{t-1} = \tilde{m}_o + \sum_{t=1}^{t-1} \frac{\eta - (p_{1b} - p_y - h_c)_t}{100 \ln (1 + \eta')} \qquad (4.6.2)$$

As emphasized above, the analysis in this chapter describes enterpreneurs' intentions. However, so far the time suffixes t and t^* for potential variables were usually deleted for reasons of convenience.

Now we will correct this omission. At the same time we assume that all relevant decisions with regard to period t are made in period t-1, hence t^{*} = t-1, and that in period t-1 all information about that period is available. Introduction of these assumptions in eq. (4.6.1) leads to:

$$a_{b_{t,t-1}} = \frac{100}{\nu_o \tilde{F}_{t-1}} (1 - \zeta_1) \tilde{h}_{c_{t,t-1}} (\tilde{i}/\tilde{y}_s)_{t-1} (1 + \eta')^{-\tilde{m}_{t-1}} +$$

$$+ \frac{(1 - \zeta_1)}{\tilde{F}_{t-1}} y_{s_{t,t-1}} - \frac{100}{\nu_o \tilde{F}_{t-1}} (1 - \zeta_1) \tilde{h}_{c_{t,t-1}} (\tilde{i}/\tilde{y}_s)_{t-1} +$$

$$+ \frac{(1 - \zeta_1)\rho}{\tilde{F}_{t-1}} - (1 - \zeta_1)\rho + (1 - \zeta_1)\mu l_{q_{t,t-1}} - (1 - \zeta_2) h_{c_{t,t-1}} +$$

$$+ \zeta_1 \overline{l_{b_{t,t-1}}} - \zeta_2 \overline{h_{c_{t,t-1}}} \qquad (4.6.3)$$

In order to meet the requirements for use of this equation and of eq. (4.6.2) for estimation purposes a number of modifications were introduced.

Both equations contain some elements for which a structural value, in the sense of some average value around a certain year, seems more relevant than the actual value for a specific year. For this reason the growth rate of potential contractual hours ($h_{c_{t,t-1}}$) was replaced by a four-year weighted average value $h_{c_{t4321}}$ which is equal to 0.4 h_{c_t} + 0.3 $h_{c_{t-1}}$ + 0.2 $h_{c_{t-2}}$ + 0.1 $h_{c_{t-3}}$.

Similarly the growth rate of potential real wages per hour in period t, $(p_{1b} - p_y - h_c)_t$ was approximated to by $(p_{1b} - p_y - h_c)_{t4321}$, and the level of the labour-income share $\tilde{F}_{t-1}$ was replaced by $\tilde{F}_{t4321}$. The level of the contractual hours $\tilde{h}_{c_{t,t-1}}$, which exhibits less fluctuation, was approximated to by the actual level $\tilde{h}_{c_t}$.

For the change in business liquidity in period t, anticipated in period t-1, $l_{q_{t,t-1}}$, we used $l_{q_{t-1}}$ as an approximation.

Introduction of these modifications, together with the approximation of the potential supply of products derived in section 4.4 (see eq. (4.4.6)) leads to:

$$a_{b_{t,t-1}} = \frac{100}{\nu_o \tilde{F}_{t4321}} (1 - \zeta_1) \tilde{h}_{c_t} (\tilde{i}/\tilde{y}_{sn})_{t-1} (1 + \eta')^{-\tilde{m}_{t-1}} +$$

$$+ \frac{(1 - \zeta_1)}{\tilde{F}_{t4321}} \left[\theta_2(y_{d_t} - \theta_4 y_{1a_t}) + (1 - \theta_2)\theta_3 - \theta_1\theta_5\tilde{q}_{t-1} \right] -$$

$$- \frac{100(1 - \zeta_1)}{\nu_o \tilde{F}_{t4321}} \tilde{h}_{c_t} (\tilde{i}/\tilde{y}_{sn})_{t-1} + \frac{(1 - \zeta_1)\rho}{\tilde{F}_{t4321}} - (1 - \zeta_1)\rho +$$

$$+ (1 - \zeta_1)\mu l_{q_{t-1}} - (1 - \zeta_2) h_{c_{t4321}} + \zeta_1 \overline{l_b}_{t,t-1} - \zeta_2 \overline{h_c}_{t,t-1} \tag{4.6.4}$$

and

$$\tilde{m}_{t-1} = \tilde{m}_o + \sum_{t=1}^{t-1} \frac{\eta - (p_{1b} - p_y - h_c)_{t4321}}{100 \ln (1 + \eta')} \tag{4.6.5}$$

5. Potential labour supply

5.1 STATISTICAL INFORMATION AND ANALYTICAL APPROACH

As a first step towards the analysis of potential labour supply we will examine the available data and hence the statistical constraints.

The total actual labour supply ($\tilde{a}_s$) consists of two components: the dependent working population ($\tilde{a}_a$) on the one hand and the conglomerate of employers, persons working on own account and unpaid family workers ($\tilde{a}_z$) on the other.
The dependent working population can be divided into: wage earners/ salaried employees ($\tilde{a}_1$) and registered unemployed ($\tilde{w}_n$).[1]
Statistical information is available (man-years, mid-year estimates) about all the above-mentioned components. The same holds for the yearly net external migration of labour supply ($\Delta\tilde{a}_m$) and net migration of frontier workers ($\Delta\tilde{a}_p$).[2]

A numerical summary of information about the Dutch labour force is given in Table 1. This table shows the interrelations for all specified labour force components and some other data such as the mean change during the sample period (1952-1970), the variance during that period and as far as appropriate the height of the corresponding level figure in the year 1960.

1. Including workers employed in additional employment programs.
2. It should be emphasized that figures about frontier workers are probably unreliable owing to registration problems.

Table 1. Survey of labour market statistics.

Except for external migration, which is specified in net yearly numbers, all descriptions and symbols refer to absolute yearly changes.

		For $\Delta\tilde{x} = \Delta\tilde{a}_1$ - - - $\Delta\tilde{a}_x$		
		Mean value of 100 $\Delta\tilde{x}/\tilde{a}_{s_{-1}}$	Variance of 100 $\Delta\tilde{x}/\tilde{a}_{s_{-1}}$	Level of $\tilde{x}$ in 1960 in 1000 man-years
Wage earners in industry	$\Delta\tilde{a}_1$	1.193	0.7337	2806
Employers, persons working on own account and unpaid family workers	$\Delta\tilde{a}_z$ +	-0.313 +	0.0046	886 +
Employment in industry	$\Delta\tilde{a}_b$	0.881	0.7450	3692
Government employment	$\Delta\tilde{a}_g$ +	0.226 +	0.0498	490 +
Total employment	$\Delta\tilde{a}_d$	1.106	0.7546	4182
Registered unemployment, including workers employed in additional employment programs	$\Delta\tilde{w}_n$ +	-0.050 +	0.3432	50 +
Total labour force	$\Delta\tilde{a}_s$	1.057	0.1790	4232
Employers etc.	$\Delta\tilde{a}_z$ -	-0.313 -	0.0046	886 -
Dependent working population	$\Delta\tilde{a}_a$	1.369	0.1662	3346
Frontier workers	$\Delta\tilde{a}_p$ -	-0.010 -	0.0039	
Dependent working population excluding frontier workers	$\Delta\tilde{a}_y$	1.380	0.1761	
Net number of external migrants with occupation	$\Delta\tilde{a}_m$ -	-0.065 -	0.0594	
Dependent working population corrected for frontier workers and external migrants	$\Delta\tilde{a}_x$	1.445	0.2319	

		For $\Delta\tilde{x} = \Delta\tilde{g}$ - - - $\Delta\tilde{g}_x$		
		Mean value of 100 $\Delta\tilde{x}/\tilde{g}_{-1}$	Variance of 100 $\Delta\tilde{x}/\tilde{g}_{-1}$	Level of $\tilde{x}$ in 1960 in 1000 man-years
Working-age population (14 - 64)	$\Delta\tilde{g}$	1.272	0.1208	7235
Net number of external migrants aged 15 - 64 [1)]	$\Delta\tilde{g}_m$ -	-0.036 -	0.0369	
Working-age population corrected for external migrants	$\Delta\tilde{g}_x$	1.308	0.0648	

1) For statistical reasons $\tilde{g}_m$ refers to the age group 15 - 64.

The table does not give a break-down of labour supply by age and sex. Such information is only available for census years (1947, 1960,1971). Hence a detailed short-term analysis of the components of labour supply, as common in American and English studies, is impossible for the Netherlands. In contrast to the situation with regard to the labour force, population figures can be broken down by age and sex for all years of the sample period. We use this information not only to compute the growth of the population in the active age classes (14-64), indicated by $\Delta\tilde{g}$, but also to approximate to the changes in labour-force participation caused by changes in the age and sex composition of the working-age population.
The additional information required for this approximation is the above-mentioned participation figures for a census year (1960). This problem is elaborated in section 5.2.2.

Other simplifications are the exogeneous treatment of the changes in the independent working population ($\Delta\tilde{a}_z$) and the changes in the working population caused by the existence of 'frontier workers', workers who live and work in different countries, indicated by $\Delta\tilde{a}_p$. As can be seen from Table 1, the relative significance of those variables in terms of the variance in total labour supply is slight. If these elements are eliminated from the total labour supply, we may rewrite the remainder in two terms: external migration of employed persons ($\Delta\tilde{a}_m$) and ($\Delta\tilde{a}_a - \Delta\tilde{a}_m - \Delta\tilde{a}_p$), for:

$$\Delta\tilde{a}_s = \Delta\tilde{a}_z + \Delta\tilde{a}_a = \Delta\tilde{a}_z + \Delta\tilde{a}_m + \Delta\tilde{a}_p + (\Delta\tilde{a}_a - \Delta\tilde{a}_m - \Delta\tilde{a}_p) \qquad (5.1.1)$$

The last term of eq. (5.1.1) may be interpreted as the growth of the dependent working population corrected for foreign influences, on the assumption that the data about external migrants and frontier workers refer to the dependent working population only.[1] For this term we will discuss an elementary approach in section 5.2. Apart

1. This assumption seems plausible for the bulk of the labour force crossing the borders.

from population growth and population composition, we assume that this term depends on real wages, hours worked and time, in such a way that the influence of the last three factors diminishes if the participation reaches saturation.

A separate treatment of the external migration of employees ($\Delta\tilde{a}_m$) will be given in section 5.3, and the results of this will be combined with those for the 'domestic' dependent working population in chapter 6.

In analogy to the treatment of labour demand in chapter 4, this chapter describes the intentions of labour suppliers, hence the analysis is generally in potential terms.

5.2 THE GROWTH OF THE DEPENDENT WORKING POPULATION CORRECTED FOR FOREIGN INFLUENCES

5.2.1 Introduction

In this section we will derive a behavioral equation for the growth of the dependent working population corrected for foreign influences in potential terms. For this purpose we define:

$$\Delta\tilde{a}_x = \Delta\tilde{a}_a - \Delta\tilde{a}_m - \Delta\tilde{a}_p \qquad (5.2.1)$$

$$\Delta\tilde{g}_x = \Delta\tilde{g} - \Delta\tilde{g}_m \qquad (5.2.2)$$

$$\tilde{r} = \tilde{a}_x/\tilde{g}_x \qquad (5.2.3)$$

where $\Delta\tilde{g}_x$ is conceived as the growth of the working-age population (14-64) corrected for foreign influences.[1] Consequently $\tilde{a}_x/\tilde{g}_x$ is to be considered as the corresponding corrected participation rate.[2]

---

1. Cf. Table 1.
2. This rate is assumed to be independent of $\tilde{a}_z/\tilde{g}_x$. No statistical evidence for a relationship between the yearly decrease of $\tilde{a}_z$ and increase of $\tilde{a}_a$ has been found.

The dependence of the changes in this participation rate on the growth and the changes in composition of the (14-64)-year population is analysed in section 5.2.2.
The rôle of other economic variables (real wages, working time, autonomous influences) is discussed in section 5.2.3, which is split up into the derivation of a basic formula (section 5.2.3.1) and the introduction of statistical modifications (5.2.3.2).
Finally, the elements of the potential labour supply corrected for foreign influences are combined in section 5.2.4.

5.2.2 Disaggregation of the participation rate by age and sex

A break-down of the 'overall' participation rate of the dependent working population by age and sex would seem to be appropriate. This break-down may be written:

$$\tilde{a}_X/\tilde{g}_X = \sum_{i=1}^{m^{*}} \tilde{g}_{X_i}/\tilde{g}_X \cdot \tilde{a}_{X_i}/\tilde{g}_{X_i} \qquad (5.2.4)$$

where m^{*} is the number of population groups.
In percentage rates of change we get from eq. (5.2.4)[1]

$$a_X - g_X = \sum_{i=1}^{m^{*}} (\tilde{a}_{X_i}/\tilde{a}_X)_{-1} (a_{X_i} - g_{X_i}) + \sum_{i=1}^{m^{*}} (\tilde{a}_{X_i}/\tilde{a}_X)_{-1} (g_{X_i} - g_X) \qquad (5.2.5)$$

By analogy with $\tilde{a}_X/\tilde{g}_X \equiv \tilde{r}$, we define $\tilde{a}_{X_i}/\tilde{g}_{X_i} \equiv \tilde{r}_i$

and rearranging the second term of eq. (5.2.5), we obtain:

$$r = a_X - g_X = \sum_{i=1}^{m^{*}} (\tilde{a}_{X_i}/\tilde{a}_X)_{-1} r_i + \frac{100}{\tilde{r}_{-1}} \cdot \sum_{i=1}^{m^{*}} \tilde{r}_{i_{-1}} \Delta(\tilde{g}_{X_i}/\tilde{g}_X) \qquad (5.2.6)$$

---

1. It should be emphasized that variables with a swung dash (∼) refer to levels, while variables without ∼ refer to percentage rates of change. Compare the introduction to the list of symbols.

The first term on the right-hand side of eq. (5.2.6) symbolizes the weighted sum of changes in the participation rates per population group as caused by other factors than changes in the composition of the (14-64)-year population. However, participation rates per population group are available only for census years. The above-mentioned change in participation is therefore treated for all groups together. This aggregated percentage rate of change in the participation rate caused by other factors than changes in population (14-64) will be indicated by r^x, which thus forms an approximation to

$$\sum_{i=1}^{m^x} (\tilde{a}_{x_i}/\tilde{a}_x)_{-1}\, r_i$$

The corresponding level figure $\tilde{r}^x$ can then be taken to represent the participation rate of the dependent working population for a constant composition of the (14-64) population e.g. in the census 1960.[1]

The next section deals with a discussion of this participation rate. The second term on the right-hand side of eq. (5.2.6) will be treated in section (5.2.3.2).

5.2.3 The determinants of the participation rate for a working-age population of a constant composition

5.2.3.1 The basic expression

Let us assume that the individual participation is dependent on real wages and working hours. We suppose furthermore that structural changes in participation may occur as a function of time. The aggregate participation ratio $\tilde{r}^x$ will accordingly show similar dependences.

Both for individuals and for the aggregate, the possibility of

1. Anglo-Saxon studies on this subject mostly deal with labour supply on more disaggregated levels and tend to separate long-run and short-run supply behaviour. For a detailed literature survey, see {27}. For an elementary approach to macro-economic potential labour supply cf. Van der Werf {41}.

increasing the labour supply would seem to be limited. Some people are not fully able to participate in production owing to social or other factors. For others it may be difficult to have more than one job. For these reasons there is some ground for the hypothesis that incentives like higher real wages have a smaller effect when the participation rate approaches an upper limit (e.g. 1).

The above-mentioned hypotheses regarding the behaviour of the labour supply have been formalized in the following equation:

$$\ln\,(\tilde{r}^{x}/\tilde{r}_s^{x})_{t,t^x} = -\,\varepsilon_1(\tilde{p}_{1b}/\tilde{p}_c)_{t,t^x}^{-\varepsilon_2}\,(\tilde{h}_c)_{t,t^x}^{\varepsilon_3}\;e^{-\varepsilon_4 t} \qquad (5.2.7)$$

where $\tilde{r}_s^{x}$: upper limit of the participation ratio

$\tilde{p}_{1b}$: wage per man paid by industry

$\tilde{p}_c$: consumption price

$\tilde{h}_c$: number of contract hours per man per year

t : (index of) reference period

t^x : period in which the decisions with regard to period t are taken

We will assume from now on that the upper limit $\tilde{r}_s^{x} = 1$. If we suppress the subindex t,t^x for the present, eq. (5.2.7) can be rewritten:

$$-\,\ln\,\tilde{r}^{x} = \varepsilon_1(\tilde{p}_{1b}/\tilde{p}_c)^{-\varepsilon_2}\,(\tilde{h}_c)^{\varepsilon_3}\;e^{-\varepsilon_4 t} \qquad (5.2.8)$$

From $0 < \tilde{r}^{x} \leqslant 1$ follows $-\ln\,\tilde{r}^{x} \geqslant 0$, so that we can take natural logarithms of eq. (5.2.8); this gives:

$$\ln(-\,\ln\,\tilde{r}^{x}) = \ln\,\varepsilon_1 - \varepsilon_2\ln\,(\tilde{p}_{1b}/\tilde{p}_c) + \varepsilon_3\ln\,(\tilde{h}_c) - \varepsilon_4 t \qquad (5.2.9)$$

Differentiating with respect to time, we obtain:

$$\frac{d\ln(-\ln \tilde{r}^{x})}{dt} = -\varepsilon_2 \frac{d\ln(\tilde{p}_{1b}/\tilde{p}_c)}{dt} + \varepsilon_3 \frac{d\ln(\tilde{h}_c)}{dt} - \varepsilon_4 \tag{5.2.10}$$

or in terms of percentage changes:

$$\frac{100}{-\ln \tilde{r}^{x}_{-1}} \cdot \frac{d(-\ln \tilde{r}^{x})}{dt} = -\varepsilon_2(p_{1b} - p_c) + \varepsilon_3(h_c) - 100\ \varepsilon_4 \tag{5.2.11}$$

or

$$r^{x} = -\varepsilon_2(\ln \tilde{r}^{x}_{-1})(p_{1b} - p_c) + \varepsilon_3(\ln \tilde{r}^{x}_{-1})(h_c) - 100\ \varepsilon_4(\ln \tilde{r}^{x}_{-1}) \tag{5.2.12}$$

Since $\varepsilon_2 > 0$ and $\varepsilon_3 > 0$ and $\ln \tilde{r}^{x}_{-1} < 0$, the percentage rate of growth is positively influenced by real wages and negatively by working hours; the relevant elasticities come closer to zero as $\tilde{r}^{x} \to 1$. The impact of the trend component on $\tilde{r}^{x}$ decreases to zero as $\tilde{r}^{x} \to 1$. We now substitute r^{x} according to eq. (5.2.12) into the first term on the right-hand side of eq. (5.2.6).

$$r = a_x - g_x = -\varepsilon_2(\ln \tilde{r}^{x}_{-1})(p_{1b} - p_c) + \varepsilon_3(\ln \tilde{r}^{x}_{-1})(h_c) - 100\ \varepsilon_4(\ln \tilde{r}^{x}_{-1}) + \frac{100}{\tilde{r}_{-1}} \sum_{i=1}^{m^{x}} \tilde{r}_{i_{-1}}\ \Delta(\tilde{g}_{x_i}/\tilde{g}_x) \tag{5.2.13}$$

5.2.3.2 Statistical modifications

A number of modifications were introduced while using eq. (5.2.13) as an estimation base.

From eq. (5.2.8) onwards the subindex t,t^{x} was suppressed. For variables not marked by a numerical subindex this means that they refer to the period t, t^{x}; variables with the suffix -1 refer to the period $t-1, t^{x}-1$. A possible reintroduction of the subindex t, t^{x} for the current potential variable r, explained by eq (5.2.13), has no consequences for the interpretation because of the assumption that the analysis generally runs in potential terms.

For the explanatory variables the situation is different. Their potential values, which are in principle required for the estimations, are not available. We therefore approximated to the relative first differences in the potential values by means of a distributed lag of the form t4321[1] on the actual relative first differences. For the levels of the explanatory values, which vary much less from year to year, the potential variables were replaced by their actual counterparts.

Next we assumed that $\ln \tilde{r}_{-1}$ comes close to $\ln \tilde{r}^{x}_{t-1,t^{x}-1}$ (during the sample period the quantitative significance of the cumulated effect of changes in the composition of the (14-64) population is negligible).

Approximations were also used with regard to the last term on the right-hand side of eq. (5.2.13).

$$\frac{100}{\tilde{r}_{-1}} \sum_{i=1}^{m^{x}} \tilde{r}_{i_{-1}} \Delta(\tilde{g}_{x_i}/\tilde{g}_x) .$$

The factor $\frac{1}{\tilde{r}_{-1}}$ can be rewritten:

---

1. Cf. list of symbols.

$$\frac{1}{\tilde{r}_{-1}} = (\tilde{g}_x/\tilde{a}_x)_{-1} = \frac{\tilde{g}_{-1} - \sum_{t=0}^{t-1} \Delta\tilde{g}_{m_t}}{\tilde{a}_{a-1} - \sum_{t=0}^{t-1} \Delta\tilde{a}_{m_t} - \sum_{t=0}^{t-1} \tilde{a}_{p_t}} \qquad (5.2.14)$$

A Σ notation has been adopted here because no obvious level figures exist with respect to net external migration and the net number of frontier workers. It would have been possible to use an arbitrarily chosen base year and to define level figures with respect to this. Because of the minor quantitative significance of both variables, however, simpler suppositions have been made.

So $\frac{1}{\tilde{r}_{-1}} = (\tilde{g}_x/\tilde{a}_x)_{-1}$ has been approximated to by $(\tilde{g}/\tilde{a}_a)_{-1}$

For lack of sufficient statistical information concerning participation rates per population group the relevant rates for 1960 have been used for $\tilde{r}_{i_{-1}}$.

To represent the changes in the (14-64) population composition we use $\Delta(\tilde{g}_i/\tilde{g})$ instead of $\Delta(\tilde{g}_{x_i}/\tilde{g}_x)$. This approximation seems justified in view of the fact that the final estimation refers to the sum of 'domestic' and 'foreign' labour supply.[1] The last term on the right-hand side of eq. (5.2.13) then takes the form:

$$\frac{100}{\tilde{r}_{-1}} \sum_{i=1}^{m^x} \tilde{r}_{i_{-1}} \Delta(\tilde{g}_{x_i}/\tilde{g}_x) = (\tilde{g}/\tilde{a}_a)_{-1} \sum_{i=1}^{m^x} \tilde{r}_{i_{60}} \Delta(\tilde{g}_i/\tilde{g}).100 \qquad (5.2.15)$$

where $\tilde{r}_{i_{60}}$ stands for the participation rate of population group i in 1960.

---

1. Cf. Chapter 6.

Analogously a_x, that is

$$\frac{\Delta\tilde{a}_x}{\tilde{a}_{x_{-1}}} = \frac{\Delta\tilde{a}_a - \Delta\tilde{a}_m - \Delta\tilde{a}_p}{\tilde{a}_{a_{-1}} - \sum_{t=0}^{t-1} \Delta\tilde{a}_{m_t} - \sum_{t=0}^{t-1} \Delta\tilde{a}_{p_t}}$$

has been approximated to by

$$\frac{\Delta\tilde{a}_a - \Delta\tilde{a}_m - \Delta\tilde{a}_p}{\tilde{a}_{a_{-1}}} = \frac{\Delta\tilde{a}_x}{\tilde{a}_{a_{-1}}} \quad ;$$

and g_x, that is

$$\frac{\Delta\tilde{g}_x}{\tilde{g}_{x_{-1}}} = \frac{\Delta\tilde{g} - \Delta\tilde{g}_m}{\tilde{g}_{-1} - \sum_{t=0}^{t-1} \Delta\tilde{g}_m}$$

by

$$\frac{\Delta\tilde{g} - \Delta\tilde{g}_m}{\tilde{g}_{-1}} = \frac{\Delta\tilde{g}_x}{\tilde{g}_{-1}}$$

5.2.4 The final expression

Substitution of the approximations mentioned in section 5.2.3.2 into eq. (5.2.13) yields:

$$(\Delta\tilde{a}_x/\tilde{a}_{a_{-1}}).100 = (\Delta\tilde{g}_x/\tilde{g}_{-1}).100 - \varepsilon_2(\ln\tilde{r}_{-1})(p_{1b} - p_c)_{t4321} +$$

$$+ \varepsilon_3(\ln\tilde{r}_{-1})(h_c)_{t4321} - 100\ \varepsilon_4(\ln\tilde{r}_{-1}) + \frac{100}{\tilde{r}_{-1}} \sum_{i=1}^{m^*} \tilde{r}_{i_{60}}\ \Delta(\tilde{g}_i/\tilde{g}) \qquad (5.2.16)$$

where $1/\tilde{r} = \tilde{g}/\tilde{a}_a$.

5.3 EXTERNAL MIGRATION

The net external migration of employed persons is the result of immigration and emigration of Dutchmen as well as foreigners. During the fifties, with Dutch emigration dominating, this figure was generally negative except for the years when Dutch immigration from Indonesia played a considerable role.
In the early sixties, however, the situation was reversed and the immigration of foreign workers into the Netherlands gradually became the principal component.
Several factors may have influenced the components of external migration in different ways. Because of the minor role net external migration plays in the variance of the total labour supply we will confine ourselves to a simple analysis. As has been shown in 5.2.3.2, a level belonging to $\Delta\tilde{a}_m$ can hardly be defined. We therefore relate the net migration of employed persons to the lagged dependent working population ($\Delta\tilde{a}_m/\tilde{a}_{a_{-1}}$); we will derive an expression for this variable in potential terms hereafter. From a theoretical point of view it would be attractive to relate the net migration of employed persons to labour conditions and other economic circumstances inside and outside the Netherlands. Such an approach would, however, require computation of economic conditions in the other countries concerned, which seems to be a labourious and disputable task. To avoid this type of difficulties we assume that the relevant change in domestic economic conditions may be represented by correcting potential domestic participation for its over-all population growth and population composition components.[1] As a

1. In theory not all determinants of domestic participation may deserve the same weight, but we neglect this complication in view of the minor numerical importance of net external migration.

short-cut solution to the representation of the changes in economic conditions outside the Netherlands, we introduce a trend factor. In this way we obtain:

$$(\Delta\tilde{a}_m/\tilde{a}_{a_{-1}}).100 = \eta_1 \left[a_x - g_x - \frac{1}{\tilde{r}_{-1}} \sum_{i=1}^{m^*} \tilde{r}_{i_{-1}} \Delta(\tilde{g}_{x_i}/\tilde{g}_x).100 \right] +$$

$$+ \eta_2 \qquad (5.3.1)$$

where η_2 is the trend-correction term.

After introduction of the approximations discussed in the previous section, eq. (5.3.1) can be rewritten:

$$(\Delta\tilde{a}_m/\tilde{a}_{a_{-1}}).100 = \eta_1 \left[(\Delta\tilde{a}_x/\tilde{a}_{a_{-1}}).100 - (\Delta\tilde{g}_x/\tilde{g}_{-1}).100 - \right.$$

$$\left. - \frac{100}{\tilde{r}_{-1}} \sum_{i=1}^{m^*} \tilde{r}_{i_{60}} \Delta(\tilde{g}_i/\tilde{g}) \right] + \eta_2 \qquad (5.3.2)$$

6. An operational labour market model

6.1 INTRODUCTION

The adaptation of model a to the approximative method treated in chapter 3 and to the analytical findings about potential labour demand and supply presented in chapters 4 and 5 leads to model c, which will be presented and discussed in section 6.2.
Based on this model, equations for the estimation of potential labour demand and supply will be derived in section 6.3.

6.2 THE LABOUR MARKET MODEL USED (MODEL C)[1]

$$a_d^p = \frac{\tilde{a}_{b_{-1}}}{\tilde{a}_{d_{-1}}} a_b^p + 100.\frac{\Delta\tilde{a}_g^p}{\tilde{a}_{d_{-1}}} \qquad (6.2.1)$$

$$a_b^p = (1 - \zeta_1).\frac{\theta_2(y_d - \theta_4 y_{1a}) + (1 - \theta_2)\theta_3 - \theta_1\theta_5\tilde{q}_{-1}}{\tilde{F}_{t4321}} +$$

$$+ 100\frac{(1 - \zeta_1)}{\nu_o}\frac{\tilde{h}_c}{\tilde{F}_{t4321}}(\tilde{i}/\tilde{y}_{sn})_{-1}\left[(1 + \eta')^{-\tilde{m}_{t-1}} - 1\right] + \rho(1-\zeta_1).$$

$$\left[\frac{1}{\tilde{F}_{t4321}} - 1\right] + \mu(1-\zeta_1)1_{q_{-1}} - (1-\zeta_2)h_{c_{t4321}} + \zeta_1\overline{1}_b^p - \zeta_2\overline{h}_c^p$$

$$(6.2.2)^a$$

1. Disturbance terms are omitted.

$$\tilde{m}_{t-1} = \tilde{m}_o + \sum_{t=1}^{t-1} \frac{\eta - (p_{1b} - p_y - h_c)_{t4321}}{100 \ln (1 + \eta')} \qquad (6.2.2)^b$$

$$\frac{\Delta\tilde{a}^p_g}{\tilde{a}_{b_{-1}}} = \frac{\Delta\tilde{a}^f_g}{\tilde{a}_{b_{-1}}} \qquad (6.2.3)$$

$$a^p_s = 100 \frac{\tilde{a}_{a_{-1}}}{\tilde{a}_{s_{-1}}} \frac{\Delta\tilde{a}^p_y}{\tilde{a}_{a_{-1}}} + 100 . \frac{\Delta\tilde{a}^p_p}{\tilde{a}_{s_{-1}}} + 100 . \frac{\Delta\tilde{a}^p_z}{\tilde{a}_{s_{-1}}} \qquad (6.2.4)$$

$$\frac{\Delta\tilde{a}^p_y}{\tilde{a}_{a_{-1}}} = \frac{\Delta\tilde{a}^p_x}{\tilde{a}_{a_{-1}}} + \frac{\Delta\tilde{a}^p_m}{\tilde{a}_{a_{-1}}} \qquad (6.2.5)$$

$$100 \frac{\Delta\tilde{a}^p_x}{\tilde{a}_{a_{-1}}} = 100 \frac{\Delta\tilde{g}_x}{\tilde{g}_{-1}} - \varepsilon_2 (\ln \tilde{r}_{-1})(p_{1b} - p_c)_{t4321} + \varepsilon_3 (\ln \tilde{r}_{-1}) h_{c_{t4321}}$$

$$- 100\ \varepsilon_4 (\ln \tilde{r}_{-1}) + \frac{100}{\tilde{r}_{-1}} \sum_{i=1}^{m^*} \tilde{r}_{i_{60}}\ \Delta\left(\frac{\tilde{g}_i}{\tilde{g}}\right) \qquad (6.2.6)$$

$$\frac{\Delta\tilde{a}^p_m}{\tilde{a}_{a_{-1}}} . 100 = \eta_1 \left[100 \frac{\Delta\tilde{a}^p_x}{\tilde{a}_{a_{-1}}} - 100 \frac{\Delta\tilde{g}_x}{\tilde{g}_{-1}} - \frac{100}{\tilde{r}_{-1}} \sum_{i=1}^{m^*} \tilde{r}_{i_{60}}\ \Delta\left(\frac{\tilde{g}_i}{\tilde{g}}\right) \right] + \eta_2 \qquad (6.2.7)$$

$$\frac{\Delta\tilde{a}^p_p}{\tilde{a}_{s_{-1}}} = \frac{\Delta\tilde{a}^f_p}{\tilde{a}_{s_{-1}}} \qquad (6.2.8)$$

$$\frac{\Delta\tilde{a}_z^p}{\tilde{a}_{s_{-1}}} = \frac{\Delta\tilde{a}_z^f}{\tilde{a}_{s_{-1}}} \tag{6.2.9}$$

$$\Delta\tilde{w}^p = a_s^p - \frac{\tilde{a}_{d_{-1}}}{\tilde{a}_{s_{-1}}} a_d^p \tag{6.2.10}$$

$$u_1^* = \phi_1^* (\tilde{a}_s^p/\tilde{a}_d^p)$$ (6.2.11) [1]

$$u_2^* = \phi_2^* (\tilde{a}_s^p/\tilde{a}_d^p)$$ (6.2.12) [1]

$$a_d^f = u_1^* a_s^p + (1 - u_1^*) a_d^p \tag{6.2.13}$$

$$a_b^f = \frac{\tilde{a}_{d_{-1}}}{\tilde{a}_{b_{-1}}} a_d^f - 100 \frac{\Delta\tilde{a}_g^f}{\tilde{a}_{b_{-1}}} \tag{6.2.14}$$

$$a_s^f = u_2^* a_s^p + (1 - u_2^*) a_d^p \tag{6.2.15}$$

$$\frac{\Delta\tilde{a}_y^f}{\tilde{a}_{a_{-1}}} \cdot 100 = \frac{\tilde{a}_{s_{-1}}}{\tilde{a}_{a_{-1}}} a_s^f - 100 \frac{\Delta\tilde{a}_p^f}{\tilde{a}_{a_{-1}}} - 100 \frac{\Delta\tilde{a}_z^f}{\tilde{a}_{a_{-1}}} \tag{6.2.16}$$

$$\Delta\tilde{w}^f = a_s^f - \frac{\tilde{a}_{d_{-1}}}{\tilde{a}_{s_{-1}}} a_d^f \tag{6.2.17}$$

---

1. These functions have been discussed in detail in chapter 3. For the choice of the parameters we refer to chapter 7.

$$\frac{\tilde{a}_s^p}{\tilde{a}_d^p} = 1 + \tilde{w}^p + \varepsilon \qquad (6.2.18)$$

$$\frac{\tilde{a}_s^f}{\tilde{a}_d^f} = 1 + \tilde{w}^f + \varepsilon' \qquad (6.2.19)$$

$$\tilde{w}^p = \sum_{t=1952}^{t} \Delta\tilde{w}_\tau^p - \frac{1}{19} \sum_{t=1952}^{1970} \sum_{t=1952}^{t} \Delta\tilde{w}_\tau^p \qquad (6.2.20)$$

$$\tilde{w}^f = \tilde{w}_{-1}^f + \Delta\tilde{w}^f \qquad (6.2.21)$$

Model c is expressed in terms of man-years (in symbols indicated by 'a'); as explained above the data required for a model in terms of man-hours per year (in symbols indicated by 'l') are lacking. Level ratios in potential terms are generally approximated to by means of denominators in actual terms. This means that every level variable in the model is in actual terms; for this reason the indication f for actual variables is omitted in the case of all level variables. In the case of changes, either f or p is added to indicate actual or potential variables respectively.

The potential and actual values of the exogeneous components of labour demand and supply (government employment, frontier workers, and the conglomerate of employers, persons working on own account and unpaid family workers - cf. equations (6.2.3), (6.2.8) and (6.2.9)- are assumed to be equal.

Total labour demand consists of demand from industry and demand from the side of the government. This shown in potential terms in eq. (6.2.1), in actual ones in eq. (6.2.14).

Industry's potential demand for labour is expressed in eq. (6.2.2)[a] which is comparable with eq. (4.6.4).

The total labour supply is composed of 3 components:

i the dependent working population, frontier workers excluded.

ii frontier workers.

iii employers, persons working on their own account and unpaid family workers.

In potential terms this is shown by eq. (6.2.4), in actual ones by eq. (6.2.16). The first component of potential labour supply is furthermore divided in the net migration of employed persons and the change in the dependent working population corrected for foreign influences. The latter change is represented by eq. (6.2.6), comparable with eq. (5.2.16), the former by eq. (6.2.7) which finds its counterpart in eq. (5.3.2).

An equation corresponding with eq. (3.1) which describes the actual demand for labour may be derived on the basis of the assumption that - measured in levels - the actual demand for labour in man-years lies between the potential demand and the potential supply (both potential variables also being expressed in man-years).

We may thus write:

$$\ln \tilde{a}_d^f = u_1 \ln \tilde{a}_s^p + (1 - u_1) \ln \tilde{a}_d^p \qquad (6.2.22)$$

Differentiating with respect to time, we obtain eq. (6.2.13), comparable with eq. (3.3^a).

Similarly, we may assume that the actual supply lies between the potential supply and the potential demand, all variables expressed in man-years. This may be written:

$$\ln \tilde{a}_s^f = u_2 \ln \tilde{a}_s^p + (1 - u_2) \ln \tilde{a}_d^p + \ln \theta \qquad (6.2.23)$$

and leads to eq. (6.2.15) along the same lines as explained above for the case of potential demand. The weights u_1^x and u_2^x depend on the ratio of potential labour demand to potential labour supply (cf. eqs. (6.2.11) and (6.2.12)), which in its turn is a function of the potential unemployment ratio, as given in eq. (6.2.18).

Eq. (6.2.19) is the counterpart of eq. (6.2.8) in actual terms. The potential unemployment ratio is determined by accumulation of its changes during the sample period. In principle, the computation of a potential unemployment ratio would require an initial level of this ratio. However, this problem is not important for our purposes. because any level could be corrected by means of the parameter ε. We therefore apply a short-cut solution: the level of the potential unemployment ratio is registered as a deviation from its mean value during the sample period. Eq. (6.2.20) describes the technical computation of the potential unemployment ratio in the sample period. The change in the unemployment ratio is by definition equal to the difference between the increase in labour supply and labour demand. Eq. (6.2.10) expresses this relation in potential terms, eq. (6.2.17) contains the same definition in actual terms.

Equations may be derived from model c for the estimation of both industry's actual demand for labour (a_b^f) and the actual supply of dependent labour, exclusive of frontier workers ($\Delta\tilde{a}_y^f/\tilde{a}_{a_{-1}}$), as will be shown in the next section.

It goes without saying that the definitional relation may be used for determination of the current level of the actual unemployment ratio, cf. eq. (6.2.21).

6.3 THE EQUATIONS TO BE ESTIMATED

6.3.1 Labour demand

Substitution of eq. (6.2.13) into eq. (6.2.14) yields:

$$a_b^f = \frac{\tilde{a}_{d_{-1}}}{\tilde{a}_{b_{-1}}} \left[u_1^x\, a_s^p + (1 - u_1^x)\, a_d^p \right] - \frac{\Delta\tilde{a}_g^f}{\tilde{a}_{b_{-1}}} \cdot 100 \qquad (6.3.1)$$

If the level of unemployment is low $\tilde{a}_d \simeq \tilde{a}_s$, so

$$a_b^f = u_1^* \frac{\Delta\tilde{a}_s^p}{\tilde{a}_{b_{-1}}} .100 + (1 - u_1^*) \frac{\Delta\tilde{a}_d^p}{\tilde{a}_{b_{-1}}} .100 - \frac{\Delta\tilde{a}_g^f}{\tilde{a}_{b_{-1}}} . 100 \qquad (6.3.2)$$

Substitution of eq. (6.2.1) and eq. (6.2.3) into (6.3.2) gives:

$$a_b^f = u_1^* \frac{\Delta\tilde{a}_s^p}{\tilde{a}_{b_{-1}}} .100 + (1 - u_1^*) \frac{\Delta\tilde{a}_b^p + \Delta\tilde{a}_g^f}{\tilde{a}_{b_{-1}}} .100 - \frac{\Delta\tilde{a}_g^f}{\tilde{a}_{b_{-1}}} .100 \qquad (6.3.3)$$

which can be reduced to:

$$a_b^f = u_1^* \frac{\Delta\tilde{a}_s^p - \Delta\tilde{a}_g^f}{\tilde{a}_{b_{-1}}} .100 + (1 - u_1^*) \frac{\Delta\tilde{a}_b^p}{\tilde{a}_{b_{-1}}} .100 \qquad (6.3.4)$$

Combination of eqs. (6.2.4), (6.2.8) and (6.2.9) yields:

$$a_b^f = u_1^* \left[\frac{\Delta\tilde{a}_y^p + \Delta\tilde{a}_p^f + \Delta\tilde{a}_z^f}{\tilde{a}_{b_{-1}}} .100 - \frac{\Delta\tilde{a}_g^f}{\tilde{a}_{b_{-1}}} .100 \right] + (1 - u_1^*)\ a_b^p \qquad (6.3.5)$$

Eq. (6.3.5) can be used as linear estimation equation by multiplying the form between brackets by u_1^* and by multiplying all elements of eq. (6.2.2^a) by $(1 - u_1^*)$.

$$a_b^f - u_1^* \left[100 . \frac{\Delta\tilde{a}_y^p + \Delta\tilde{a}_p^f + \Delta\tilde{a}_z^f}{\tilde{a}_{b_{-1}}} - 100 . \frac{\Delta\tilde{a}_g^f}{\tilde{a}_{b_{-1}}} \right] =$$

$$= \beta_1(1 - u_1^*) \frac{y_d - \theta_4 y_{1a}}{\tilde{F}_{t4321}} + \beta_2(1 - u_1^*) \frac{\tilde{q}_{-1}}{\tilde{F}_{t4321}} + \frac{\beta_3(1 - u_1^*)}{\tilde{F}_{t4321}} +$$

$$+ \beta_4(1 - u_1^*) \frac{\tilde{h}_c}{\tilde{F}_{t4321}} (\tilde{i}/\tilde{y}_{sn})_{-1} . 100 \left[(1 + \eta')^{-\tilde{m}_{t-1}} - 1 \right] +$$

$$+ \beta_5(1 - u_1^*) l_{q_{-1}} + \beta_6(1 - u_1^*) h_{c_{t4321}} + \beta_7(1 - u_1^*) \qquad (6.3.6)$$

where

$$\tilde{m}_{t-1} = \tilde{m}_o + \sum_{t=1}^{t-1} \frac{\eta - (p_{1b} - p_y - h_c)_{t4321}}{100 \ln (1 + \eta')} \qquad (6.3.7)$$

and the parameters to be estimated are:

$$\beta_1 = \theta_2(1 - \zeta_1) \qquad (6.3.6^a)$$

$$\beta_2 = - (1 - \zeta_1)\theta_1\theta_5 \qquad (6.3.6^b)$$

$$\beta_3 = (1 - \zeta_1) \left[(1 - \theta_2)\theta_3 + \rho \right] \qquad (6.3.6^c)$$

$$\beta_4 = \frac{1 - \zeta_1}{\nu_o} \qquad (6.3.6^d)$$

$$\beta_5 = \mu(1 - \zeta_1) \qquad (6.3.6^e)$$

$$\beta_6 = - (1 - \zeta_2) \qquad (6.3.6^f)$$

$$\beta_7 = - \rho(1 - \zeta_1) + \zeta_1 \bar{l}_b^p - \zeta_2 \bar{h}_c^p \qquad (6.3.6^g)$$

6.3.2 Labour supply

Similar expressions can be derived for the labour supply. Substitution of eq. (6.2.15) into eq. (6.2.16) yields:

$$\frac{\Delta\tilde{a}^f_y}{\tilde{a}_{a_{-1}}}.100 = \frac{\tilde{a}_{s_{-1}}}{\tilde{a}_{a_{-1}}}\left[u_2^* \, a_s^p + (1 - u_2^*) \, a_d^p\right] - \frac{\Delta\tilde{a}^f_p}{\tilde{a}_{a_{-1}}}.100 - \frac{\Delta\tilde{a}^f_z}{\tilde{a}_{a_{-1}}}.100 \tag{6.3.8}$$

Using $\tilde{a}_d \simeq \tilde{a}_s$ again, we find:

$$\frac{\Delta\tilde{a}^f_y}{\tilde{a}_{a_{-1}}} = u_2^* \frac{\Delta\tilde{a}^p_s}{\tilde{a}_{a_{-1}}} + (1 - u_2^*) \frac{\Delta\tilde{a}^p_d}{\tilde{a}_{a_{-1}}} - \frac{\Delta\tilde{a}^f_p + \Delta\tilde{a}^f_z}{\tilde{a}_{a_{-1}}} \tag{6.3.9}$$

Substitution of eqs. (6.2.4), (6.2.8) and (6.2.9) into eq. (6.3.9) yields:

$$\frac{\Delta\tilde{a}^f_y}{\tilde{a}_{a_{-1}}} = u_2^* \frac{\Delta\tilde{a}^p_y + \Delta\tilde{a}^f_p + \Delta\tilde{a}^f_z}{\tilde{a}_{a_{-1}}} + (1 - u_2^*) \frac{\Delta\tilde{a}^p_d}{\tilde{a}_{a_{-1}}} - \frac{\Delta\tilde{a}^f_p + \Delta\tilde{a}^f_z}{\tilde{a}_{a_{-1}}} \tag{6.3.10}$$

or

$$\frac{\Delta\tilde{a}^f_y}{\tilde{a}_{a_{-1}}} = u_2^* \frac{\Delta\tilde{a}^p_y}{\tilde{a}_{a_{-1}}} + (1 - u_2^*) \left[\frac{\Delta\tilde{a}^p_d}{\tilde{a}_{a_{-1}}} - \frac{\Delta\tilde{a}^f_p + \Delta\tilde{a}^f_z}{\tilde{a}_{a_{-1}}}\right] \tag{6.3.11}$$

Substitution of eqs. (6.2.1), (6.2.3) and (6.2.5) into eq. (6.3.11) gives:

$$\frac{\Delta \tilde{a}^f_y}{\tilde{a}_{a_{-1}}} = u_2^* \frac{\Delta \tilde{a}^p_x + \Delta \tilde{a}^p_m}{\tilde{a}_{a_{-1}}} + (1 - u_2^*) \left[\frac{\Delta \tilde{a}^p_b + \Delta \tilde{a}^f_g}{\tilde{a}_{a_{-1}}} - \frac{\Delta \tilde{a}^f_p + \Delta \tilde{a}^f_z}{\tilde{a}_{a_{-1}}} \right] \tag{6.3.12}$$

This equation is the basis for the supply estimations presented in this study. Substitution of eqs. (6.2.6) and (6.2.7) into it yields:

$$100 \frac{\Delta \tilde{a}^f_y}{\tilde{a}_{a_{-1}}} - 100 \, (1 - u_2^*) \left[\frac{\Delta \tilde{a}^p_b + \Delta \tilde{a}^f_g}{\tilde{a}_{a_{-1}}} - \frac{\Delta \tilde{a}^f_p + \Delta \tilde{a}^f_z}{\tilde{a}_{a_{-1}}} \right]$$

$$- 100 \, u_2^* \frac{\Delta \tilde{g}_x}{\tilde{g}_{-1}} - \frac{u_2^*}{\tilde{r}_{-1}} \sum_{i=1}^{m^*} \tilde{r}_{i_{60}} \, 100 \, \Delta(\frac{\tilde{g}_i}{\tilde{g}}) =$$

$$= \varepsilon_5 \, u_2^* \, (\ln \tilde{r}_{-1})(p_{1b} - p_c)_{t4321} + \varepsilon_6 \, u_2^* \, (\ln \tilde{r}_{-1}) h_{c_{t4321}} +$$

$$+ \varepsilon_7 \, u_2^* \, (\ln \tilde{r}_{-1}) + \eta_2 \, u_2^* \tag{6.3.13}$$

where the parameters to be estimated are:

$$\varepsilon_5 = - (1 + \eta_1) \varepsilon_2 \tag{6.3.13^a}$$

$$\varepsilon_6 = (1 + \eta_1) \varepsilon_3 \tag{6.3.13^b}$$

$$\varepsilon_7 = - 100 \, (1 + \eta_1) \varepsilon_4 \tag{6.3.13^c}$$

and η_2

7. Application of the model

7.1 INTRODUCTION

This chapter describes the empirical part of our study. As an introduction to the actual estimations based on the equations (6.3.6) and (6.3.13) the statistical representation of variables is elaborated in section 7.2 and the preliminary determination of some, mostly non-linear, parameters and the age of the oldest capital goods with respect to the base year is discussed in section 7.3. Section 7.4 deals with some technical details of the estimation procedure. The regression results are reviewed in section 7.5. The over-all results of the estimation are evaluated on the basis of a comparison of actual and potential variables in section 7.6.

7.2 STATISTICAL REPRESENTATION OF VARIABLES

After the discussion of the available labour market statistics in chapter 4 and 5, a very brief discussion of the quantitative representation of eqs. (6.3.6) and (6.3.13) will suffice here. Among other things, we used the following data based on the Dutch National Accounts 1970:

y_d : yearly percentage rate of change of the volume of production of enterprises (gross market prices)

y_{1a} : the difference between the actual growth rate of agricultural production and its average growth rate during the sample period

$\tilde{F}$: the share of labour in the total national income computed by imputing to independent workers the same income from labour as dependent workers (gross market prices)

$\tilde{q}$: the excess capacity, expressed as a percentage of the one-year lagged capacity level as approximated to by C.A. van den Beld {6} (as deviation from its mean value during the sample period)

$\tilde{h}_c$: the approximate index of average contractual working hours per man in industry

$\tilde{i}$: the volume of investment in equipment of enterprises, excluding vessels and airplanes

$\tilde{y}_{sn}$: 0.968 $\tilde{cap}$, where $\tilde{cap}$ is the capacity level referred to above; the factor 0.968 is the approximate average ratio of potential product supply to production capacity in the sample period[1]

l_q : yearly rate of change of the liquidity ratio of industry as defined in section 4.4.2

p_{lb} : yearly rate of change of wages per worker paid by enterprises[2]

p_c : yearly rate of change of price of private consumption

h_c : approximate yearly rate of change in the average contractual hours per man in industry.

---

1. The average capacity surplus in the sample period is 3.3%. We assume $\overline{w} \sim 0$ and $\overline{s} \sim 0$ for this period. With this assumption, it follows that $\bar{\tilde{y}}^p_d \sim \bar{\tilde{y}}^f_d$. Hence $\bar{\tilde{y}}^p_{sn} = \bar{\tilde{y}}^p_d = \bar{\tilde{y}}^f_d = 0.968\ \tilde{cap}$.
2. We neglected any possible influence of a difference between government wages and wages paid by industrial enterprises as a cause of supply changes. The prevailing system of government wage determination in the Netherlands tends to eliminate these wage differences.

7.3 PREDETERMINATION OF PARAMETERS AND BASIC VALUES

Apart from the statistical representation of elements in the estimation equations, other numerical values have to be introduced in order to adapt the equations to the requirements for linear regression.

As anticipated in chapter 4, no statistics are available for the initial age of the oldest vintage in use $\tilde{m}_o$. We therefore chose an <u>a priori</u> value for this quantity after some trial and error, which we performed at the same time as the introduction of alternative values for the growth rate of labour productivity per vintage (η). The dependence of the investment ratio on alternative values for both $\tilde{m}_o$ and η is shown in appendix D. It is worth-while noting that the wish to estimate interpretable parameters for the demand equation leaves little room for the variation in $\tilde{m}_o$ and η. An interesting check on the consistency of the results is discussed in section 7.5.1. A statistical problem is the low variance of $(1/\tilde{F}_{4321})$. Difficulties to be expected from a simultaneous estimation of β_3 and β_7 are avoided by conditioning the value of β_7. We found by trial and error that $\beta_7 = -1.1$ is probably the best value.

Another predetermined coefficient is θ_4. Its value is fixed at 0.1 on the basis of the ratio between the coefficients of y_d and y_{1a} in estimations where these variables occurred separately.

A special predetermination problem is the choice of the parameters α, β, γ, δ and ε, essential for the computation of the weights u_1^* and u_2^*. The parameters ultimately chosen are presented in Appendix E. The estimation of labour demand generally seems to require low-average, high-dispersion weights while estimation of the labour supply benefits from high-average, low-dispersion weights. The economic interpretation of the weights chosen has been discussed in chapter 3. Statistically the variation of weights leaves some room for the manipulation of the variance of the potential variables, especially in the case of potential labour demand. On the other hand the accumulated level of the potential unemployment ratio seems

rather insensitive to (modest) variations in u_1^x and u_2^x.
In the first round the weights are based on the actual labour demand/supply ratio, and applied to the actual labour supply in the labour demand equation and to the actual labour demand in the labour supply equation. In the second round therefore the parameters may have to be adapted. After the second round, there is no longer any need to change parameters.
The choice of ε, the correction term for the difference between sample-average unemployment and equilibrium unemployment, deserves special attention. For the first round the actual average unemployment ratio of 1.52% was corrected by 0.0165 to get a sample period difference from equilibrium unemployment of - 0.13%.[1]
For the second and later rounds the average of Q fixed by the computation method was corrected by ε = -0.002 to get an average deviation from potential equilibrium unemployment of -0.2%.

7.4 THE ESTIMATION PROCEDURE

The estimations presented below are based on eq. (6.3.6) for labour demand and eq. (6.3.13) for labour supply.
As indicated in chapter 3 the first-round weights are based on the actual unemployment rate. In this round the term $(\Delta\tilde{a}_y^p/\tilde{a}_{b_{-1}})$ in eq. (6.3.6) was replaced by $(\Delta\tilde{a}_y^f/\tilde{a}_{b_{-1}})$ and similarly in eq. (6.3.13) $(\Delta\tilde{a}_b^p/\tilde{a}_{a_{-1}})$ by $(\Delta\tilde{a}_b^f/\tilde{a}_{a_{-1}})$.
The first-round parameter estimates enable us to compute potential values of $(\Delta\tilde{a}_y^p/\tilde{a}_{b_{-1}})$, $(\Delta\tilde{a}_y^p/\tilde{a}_{a_{-1}})$ and $\Delta\tilde{w}^p$.
This makes it possible to compute weights based on potential unemployment from the first round to be used in the second round. New

1. In the period 1952-1970 there was some net emigration (cf. Table 1). For years in which $\tilde{w}$ > 1.8% the emigration surplus was positive, for $\tilde{w}$ < 1.5% it was negative in this period. ε was assumed to be -1.65% in the first round. The actual and corrected values of the unemployment ratio may be derived from Table 4.

estimations were then set up for the eqs. (6.3.6) and (6.3.13), and so on. After some rounds the regression coefficients do stabilize. The ultimate regression results will be discussed in the next sections.

7.5 THE ESTIMATION RESULTS

The results of the estimations based on eqs. (6.3.6) and (6.3.13) are presented in Table 2 for various stages of the calculation, while the final results are shown in Fig. 2 and 3. The estimation results changed considerably from round 1 to round 2, as may be seen from Table 2. After the second round the changes were relatively small, and after the seventh round they were negligible.
A consistent solution for model c was thus obtained in seven rounds. The ultimate results can be dealt with in several ways. We will start by discussing the final estimated regression coefficients in section 7.5.1 (demand) and 7.5.2 (supply).

7.5.1 Labour demand

The structural parameters θ_1, θ_2, θ_3, θ_5, ζ_1, ζ_2, μ and ν_o cannot all be identified unless some additional assumptions are made. We will derive below the values of the other parameters for an assumed value of 1 for the capital-output ratio in the base year (ν_o).
Eq. (6.3.6^f) gives directly $\zeta_2 = 1 + \beta_6 = 0.265.$[1]
Substitution of $\nu_o = 1$ into eq. (6.3.6^d) yields:

$$\zeta_1 = 1 - \beta_4 = 0.410 .$$

We next compute $\theta_2 = \dfrac{\beta_1}{1 - \zeta_1} = 0.269$ and $\mu = \dfrac{\beta_5}{1 - \zeta_1} = 0.161$

1. All parameters are presented to 3 places of decimals; small deviations may result from the fact that the computations are carried out to more places of decimals.

from eqs. (6.3.6^a) and (6.3.6^e) respectively.

It follows from eq. (6.3.6^b) that $\theta_1\theta_5 = \dfrac{-\beta_2}{1-\zeta_1} = 0.442.$

We can now solve eq. (6.3.6^g) for ρ:

$$\rho = \frac{-\beta_7 + \zeta_1\,\bar{l}^p_b - \zeta_2\,\bar{h}^p_c}{1-\zeta_1} \quad .$$

If we approximate to $\bar{l}^{p}_b$[1] by 0.60 and to $\bar{h}^{p}_c$[1] by -0.46, the rate of technical deterioration of machinery (ρ) equals 2.488%.
Finally θ_3 follows from eq. (6.3.6^c):

$$\theta_3 = \frac{\beta_3}{(1-\zeta_1)(1-\theta_2)} - \frac{\rho}{(1-\theta_2)} = 6.174\% \quad .$$

In order to check the plausibility of some of these coefficients we may insert them in the structural relations.
In the case of μ eq. (4.4.8) becomes:

$$l_{b_t} = l_t + 0.161\ l_{q_t} \quad .$$

There seems to be no reason why we should not accept this elasticity. Eq. (4.4.6) now transforms into:

$$y_{sc_{t,t-1}} = 0.269\ (y_{d_t} - 0.1\ y_{1a_t}) - 0.442\ \tilde{q}_{t-1} + 4.513 \quad .$$

---

1. If we assume - for lack of other information - $\bar{h}^p_c$ to be equal to the actual average value of $h_{c_{t4321}}$ over the sample period and $\bar{o}^p_b = 0$, we may derive:
$\bar{l}^p_b = \bar{a}^p_b + \bar{h}^p_c + \bar{o}^p_b = 1.06 - 0.46 = 0.60$.

This result implies a growth of potential current supply of products over the sample period at an average rate of about 6% per year, assuming the average tension on the product market to be zero, and $y_d^p = 5.60\%$.[1]
This growth rate is somewhat higher than the actual capacity growth, which was estimated by Van den Beld to be 5.00% per year on the average. However, we cannot exclude the possibility that the increase in the potential supply of products exceeded the actual supply increase considerably in the sample period.[2]
The value of $\theta_1\theta_5$ can be split up conditionally. From Siebrand {33} we borrow $\theta_5 \simeq 1.5$ which implies $\theta_1 = 0.295$. This result means that it is expected that an existing excess supply of products in the decision period will be reduced by almost 30% in the reference period.
The coefficients ζ_1 and ζ_2 occur in eq. (4.5.3); their computed values lead to:

$$o_b = 0.410\ (l_b - \bar{l}_b^p) - 0.265\ (h_c - \bar{h}_c^p) \quad .$$

This implies that an increase in labour demand in man-hours per year in excess of the average increase is absorbed by somewhat more than 40% in the short-term by an increase in overtime, and a decrease in contractual working hours is compensated by about 25% by an increase in overtime. The combination of the derived value of ρ (technical deterioration) with the assumptions about the age composition of the capital stock enables us to carry out an interesting consistency check on our assumptions and results. Together with the data on investment outlays for 1969 and earlier, this information determines the volume of the capital stock in 1970. As demon-

---

1. This assumption is based on an earlier study by the second author {33}.
2. It should be remembered that this is a conditional result. Alternative assumptions would lead to different results; we will come back to this point later in this section.

Table 2. Estimation results.

	ROUND 1	ROUND 2	ROUND 7
DEMAND			
β_1 (production)	0.152	0.159	0.159
	(4.0)	(4.4)	(4.5)
β_2 (excess capacity)	-0.259	-0.259	-0.261
	(-6.8)	(-6.6)	(-6.7)
β_3 (labour income share)	4.339	4.126	4.131
	(5.3)	(5.0)	(5.1)
β_4 (investment ratio)	0.618	0.588	0.590
	(5.2)	(4.9)	(5.0)
β_5 (liquidity)	0.089	0.093	0.095
	(3.1)	(3.3)	(3.5)
β_6 (contract hours)	-0.862	-0.713	-0.735
	(-3.0)	(-2.8)	(-3.0)
β_7 (constant)	-1.100	-1.100	-1.100
	(-)	(-)	(-)
VAR U	0.066	0.088	0.085
R^2	0.935	0.931	0.933
DW	2.037	2.252	2.262
SUPPLY			
ε_5 (wages)	-0.354	-0.393	-0.385
	(-3.1)	(-3.6)	(-3.6)
ε_6 (contract hours)	0.416	0.367	0.394
	(2.3)	(2.1)	(2.3)
ε_7 (participation rate)	-27.702	-28.969	-29.133
	(-5.5)	(-6.0)	(-6.1)
η_2 (constant)	-22.472	-23.592	-23.693
	(-5.3)	(-5.7)	(-5.8)
VAR U	0.048	0.061	0.060
R^2	0.679	0.718	0.727
DW	2.453	2.528	2.516

Fig. 2 Demand Estimation

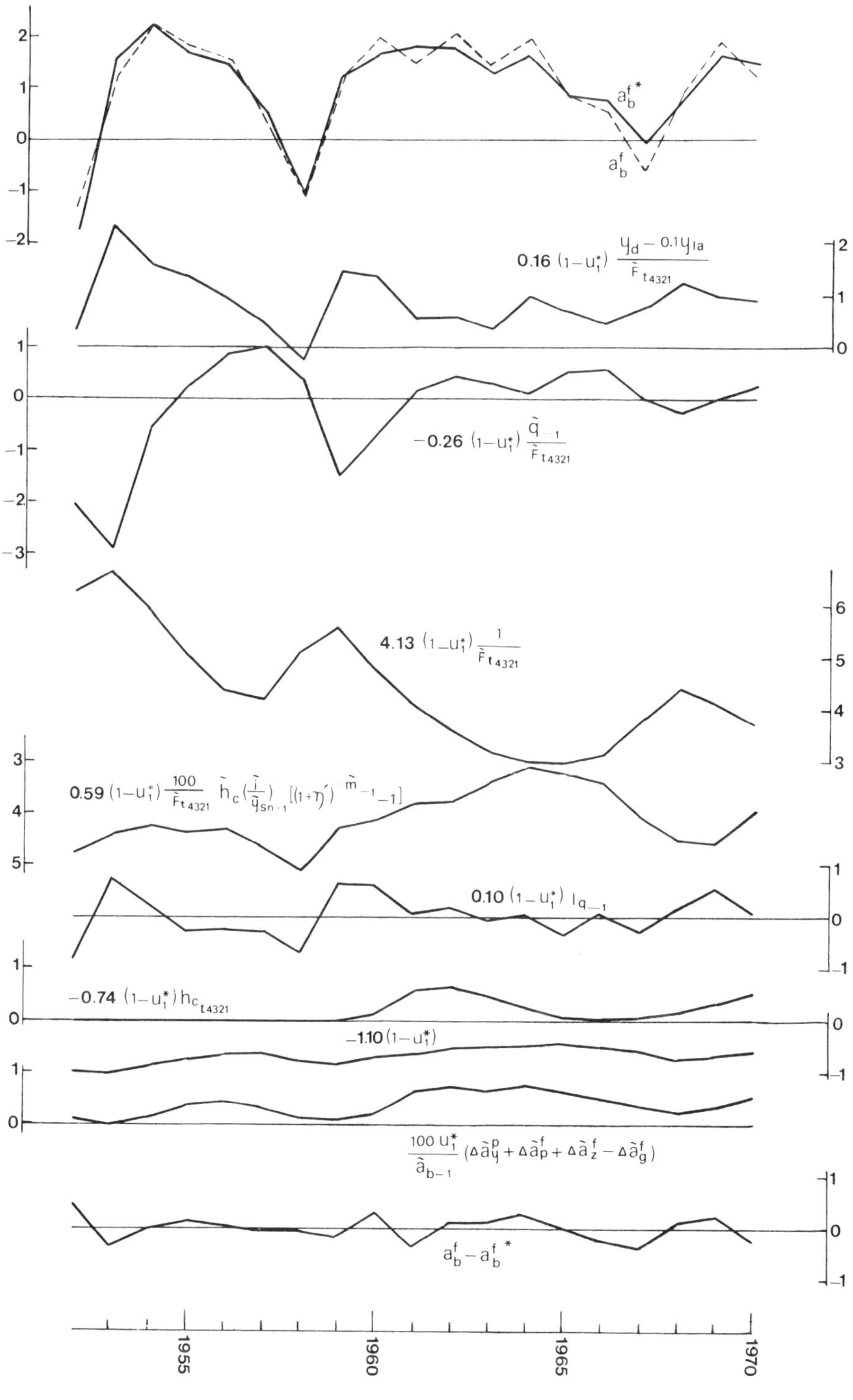

Fig.3 Supply Estimation

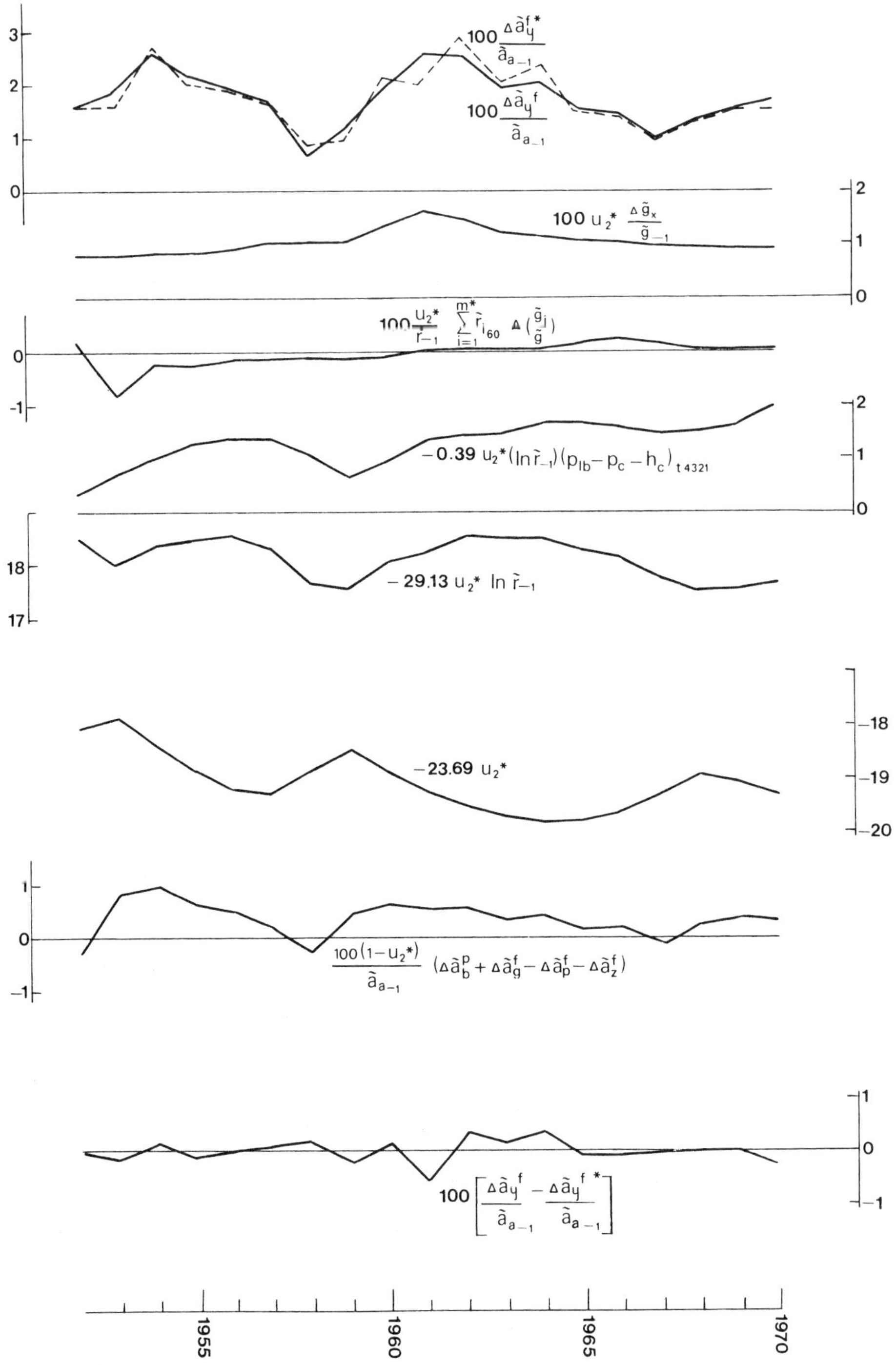

strated in appendix F the resulting capital stock in 1970 (in 1963 prices) is 80.0 (mld guilders).
On the other hand, the capital stock may be computed on the basis of the assumed capital output ratio and the production capacity in 1970; with $\nu_{51} = 1$, eq. (4.5.6) gives:

$$\nu_{70} = \tilde{h}^{-1}_{c_{70}} . \nu_{51} = 1.109. \text{ Hence } \tilde{k}_{70} = 1.109\ \tilde{y}_{sn_{70}} =$$

$$= 1.109 \ .\ 0.968 \ .\ \tilde{cap}_{70} = 78.5 \text{ (mld of guilders).}$$ [1]

The difference between this value and 80.0 is very small, but we must not forget that this is a conditional result. Once we assume $\nu_o \neq 1$, the agreement may be much worse. If e.g. we assume - in contrast with our present results - that the growth of potential supply of products ($\tilde{y}_{sc}$) is equal to the growth of the production capacity in the sample period, the accumulated capital stock tends to be less than the capital stock required according to the capital-output ratio. This inconsistency may be removed by additional assumptions such as that the labour-income as used here exceeds the marginal labour productivity[2] In general terms we may conclude that a clay-clay production function of the type we use seems only able to explain the actual average employment growth in the sample period if we make assumptions that tend to increase labour demand such as a greater growth of intended product supply than that of actual product supply or a lower labour productivity than labour income suggests. The implications of these alternative hypotheses are very interesting: the question as to whether employment growth in the period 1951 to 1970 was that big because of ambitious product supply

1. The ratio of $\tilde{y}_{sn_{70}}$ to $\tilde{cap}_{70}$ is based on the average ratio, as explained earlier in this section.
2. In view of the structural withdrawal of the self-employed one may question the equality of their productivity and the productivity of the average member of the dependent labour force.

schemes or because of e.g. a continuous attempt of entrepreneurs to substitute over-paid workers for machinery by means of high investments in an environment conditioned by rigid production relations, seems to be of much practical importance. One might speculate that for the fifties the first assumption was more realistic, while the second assumption was dominant in the sixties. Whatever the case a discussion of this interesting issue is beyond the scope of this study. The t-values of the coefficients of the labour demand estimation have an acceptable level, and the explanatory power of the equation for the sample period is rather high.[1]

An interesting, and in view of the current development of unemployment in the Netherlands even dramatic issue is the question as to which factors determine the average growth rate of employment in a medium-term setting. It is not easy to solve this problem for our sample period. Of course, eq. (6.3.5) enables us to compute the average contribution of the growth rates of potential labour demand and potential labour supply to the growth rate of actual labour demand for the period 1951 - 1970 in the following way:

$$\frac{1}{19}\sum_{1952}^{1970}(1-u_1^{*})\,a_b^p = 0.62$$

$$\frac{1}{19}\sum_{1952}^{1970}u_1^{*}.100\,\frac{\Delta\tilde{a}_y^p+\Delta\tilde{a}_p^f+\Delta\tilde{a}_z^f-\Delta\tilde{a}_g^f}{\tilde{a}_{b_{-1}}} = 0.40$$

$$\bar{a}_b^f = 1.02$$

1. It is interesting to note that the expression for the potential labour demand explains the actual employment growth in the sample period even better if the quality is judged in terms of residual variance and coefficients of determination. The coefficients of the 'unweighted' variables and their t-values are: β_1=0.13 (9.3), β_2=-0.19 (11.0), β_3=3.06 (8.9), β_4=0.41 (7.9) β_5=0.07 (6.1), β_6=-0.52(5.7), β_7=-1.10 (-) Var U=0.039 R^2=0.972 DW=2.306

However, the weights u_1^x and $(1-u_1^x)$ depend on the growth rates of potential labour demand and potential labour supply as well. In principle we could calculate the contribution of e.g. the growth of potential labour demand by recomputing the weights for a zero growth rate of potential labour supply for any year, etc,. but this would require substantial calculations, possibly yielding little crucial information, since the actual difference between the average growth rates of potential labour demand (1.06) and that of actual labour demand (1.02) is very small. It therefore seems permissible to concentrate on the contribution of the potential labour demand to the growth rate for an approximation to the demand factors behind the growth of actual employment.
The details of this argument are discussed in appendix G, and the results are summarized in Table 3.
Over the whole period the impact of net investment explains almost half of the potential employment growth. The change in working hours - which we assumed to be combined with an equal change in machine operating time - accounts for somewhat more than half. The effect of changes in business liquidity is very slight. However, the effects are far from evenly distributed over the sub-periods in question. In particular, the fast increase in the impact of economic obsolescence, due to a rapid increase in real wages, is responsible for a vanishing impact of net investment on potential employment after 1957. The increase of this factor from the second to the third period is just compensated by an increase in gross investment caused by an acceleration in the growth of intended product supply (technically due to the production and excess-capacity variable). Corrected for the somewhat incidental monetary influences, the growth rate of potential employment shows a continued decrease over the sub-periods, and - perhaps more important - the growth of potential employment in man-years after 1957 is almost completely caused by a change in hours worked per man. In other words, after correction for the effects of changes in business liquidity, which by their nature are temporary, the change in

Table 3. [1)]

Average impacts on potential employment (exclusive of overtime effects).

Periods:	1951-1970		1951-1957		1957-1963		1963-1970	
Determinants:								
Gross investment (newly installed machinery)		5.76		5.06		5.43		6.64
Economic obsolescence	-2.80		-1.17		-2.90		-4.11	
Technical deterioration	-2.49		-2.49		-2.49		-2.49	
Total depreciation		-5.29		-3.66		-5.39		-6.60
Net investment		0.47		1.40		0.04		0.04
Liquidity		0.04		-0.28		0.36		0.05
Contractual working hours		0.46		0.00		0.80		0.54
Machine operating time		0.07		0.00		0.12		0.08
(Growth rate of potential employment)		1.04 [2)]		1.12		1.32		0.71

1) Our results agree remarkably well with those of Tjan Hok Soei and H. den Hartog in a medium-term analysis {18} based on a similar production function. In the Netherlands this study from the Central Planning Bureau gave rise to a passionate discussion on the relevance of real wages to the present employment problem.

2) The difference between this value and the above-mentioned average growth rate of potential employment (1.06) is due to rounding-off.

employment in terms of man-hours per year virtually came to a standstill in the sixties in the Netherlands.

7.5.2 Labour supply

In the case of labour supply the coefficient of determination is much lower, but due to the small variance of potential labour supply compared with that of potential labour demand the residual variance is lower too.[1]

The evaluation of the coefficients is somewhat less exact because of thc impossibility of identifying the structural coefficients, except for η_2.

The estimated values of ε_5, ε_6, ε_7 and η_2 are presented in Table 2. The coefficient η_2 has a rather high negative nalue (-23.693), but in order to study the trendwise change in potential labour supply caused by both external migration and domestic factors we should combine this partial influence with the trend influence incorporated in the term $\varepsilon_7 \ln \tilde{r}_{-1}$. For the average value of $\ln \tilde{r}_{-1}$ which is -0.775 the total trend factor is $-23.693 - [29.133.(-0.775)] = -1.115$.

This total cannot be divided into a 'domestic' and a 'foreign' component because η_1 is underidentified.[2]

The absolute values of the elasticities with respect to real wages and contractual working hours are equal. Hence, we may compute the average elasticity of labour supply with respect to real hourly wages. Its value is $-0.39.(-0.775) = 0.30$.

---

1. Both the labour demand and supply estimations of course, depend on the selected weights. Both in the case of demand and in the case of supply a change in the weights tends to affect the variation in the growth rates of the potential items, but leaves the average growth rates over the period 1951-1970 and the average level of the potential unemployment ratio practically unchanged.
2. As far as the 'foreign' labour supply is concerned some negative trend may be expected, representing emigration in the case of constant Dutch wages and working hours caused by the rate of improvement of economic conditions outside the Netherlands.

At the end of the sample period this elasticity was about 10% lower than in the beginning. This result seems acceptable.
In the case of ε_7 it is interesting to calculate the difference between the highest and the lowest trend contributions to actual supply growth caused by different levels of the participation rate. The highest contribution to the trend rate of growth was 18.5 in 1952, and the lowest was 17.7 in 1970. The difference (after rounding-off) is 0.8(%).
The average contributions to the growth of potential labour supply over the sample period are:

$\varepsilon_5 \ln \tilde{r}_{-1} (p_{1b} - p_c)_{t4321}$	1.47	('wages')
$\varepsilon_6 \ln \tilde{r}_{-1} h_{c_{t4321}}$	0.14 +	('working hours')
	1.61	('wages per hour')
$\varepsilon_7 \ln \tilde{r}_{-1} + \eta_2$	-1.12	('trend')
$\frac{\Delta \tilde{g}_x}{\tilde{g}_{-1}} \cdot 100$	1.31	('population growth')
$\frac{100}{\tilde{r}_{-1}} \sum_{i=1}^{m^*} \tilde{r}_{i_{60}} \Delta(\frac{\tilde{g}_i}{\tilde{g}})$	-0.07 +	('population composition')
$\frac{\Delta \tilde{a}^p_y}{\tilde{a}_{a_{-1}}} \cdot 100$	1.73	('potential supply')

According to eq. (6.3.12) the average growth rate of actual supply over the period 1951-1970 may be considered as composed of the weighted average growth rates of potential labour supply and potential labour demand. This yields:

$$\frac{1}{19} \sum_{1952}^{1970} u_2^{*} \, 100 \, \frac{\Delta \tilde{a}_y^p}{\tilde{a}_{a_{-1}}} = 1.39$$

$$\frac{1}{19} \sum_{1952}^{1970} (1 - u_2^{*})(100. \frac{\Delta \tilde{a}_b^p + \Delta \tilde{a}_g^f - \Delta \tilde{a}_p^f - \Delta \tilde{a}_z^f}{\tilde{a}_{a_{-1}}}) = 0.37$$

$$+$$

$$100. \frac{\Delta \tilde{a}_y^f}{\tilde{a}_{a_{-1}}} = 1.76$$

However, like in the case of demand, this result contains weights which are dependent on the growth rates of potential demand and supply.

7.6 EVALUATION

In order to permit comparison of the estimated potential variables with the corresponding actual variables, Table 4 and Fig. 4 give both values and the difference between them for

a) employment in industry

b) labour supply (excluding self-employed and frontier workers)

c) the changes in the unemployment ratio

d) the level of the unemployment ratio

The common opinion that the fluctuations in the tension on the labour market are largely demand-determined is reflected in the figure.

Potential labour demand shows a more violent fluctuation then actual demand; this is particularly clear for boom and recession years, and is also shown by a comparison of the variances of both series and confirmed by the regression result:[1]

$$a_b^{p^*} = 1.30\, a_b^f - 0.26 \qquad \text{VAR U} \quad R^2 \quad \text{DW}$$
$$(22.5) \qquad (-3.1) \qquad 0.061 \quad 0.967 \quad 2.241$$

The average growth rate of potential labour demand is slightly higher than that of actual labour demand, while for the average growth rate of potential labour supply the reverse holds; these deviations appear to be consistent. The potential labour supply grew more smoothly than its actual counterpart. Regression gives:

$$100.\frac{\Delta \tilde{a}_y^{p^*}}{\tilde{a}_{a_{-1}}} = 0.57(100)\frac{\Delta \tilde{a}_y^f}{\tilde{a}_{a_{-1}}} + 0.73 \qquad \text{VAR U} \quad R^2 \quad \text{DW}$$
$$(4.5) \qquad (3.1) \qquad 0.090 \quad 0.543 \quad 1.930$$

A negative correlation is to be expected between the difference between potential labour demand and actual labour demand on the one hand and the difference between potential labour supply and actual labour supply on the other. This is confirmed by the regression result:[2]

$$a_b^{p^*} - a_b^f = -0.56(100)\left(\frac{\Delta \tilde{a}_y^{p^*}}{\tilde{a}_{a_{-1}}} - \frac{\Delta \tilde{a}_y^f}{\tilde{a}_{a_{-1}}}\right) \qquad \text{VAR U} \quad R^2 \quad \text{DW}$$
$$(-2.8) \qquad 0.106 \quad 0.299 \quad 2.077$$

Because adaptation of labour demand and supply tends to damp the pressure of labour demand, both the changes and the level of the potential unemployment ratio should show a bigger variance than the corresponding figures for actual unemployment. This is also con-

1. Estimated variables are indicated by an asterisk (x)
2. Insignificant constants were suppressed.

Fig.4 Comparison Potential and Actual Variables

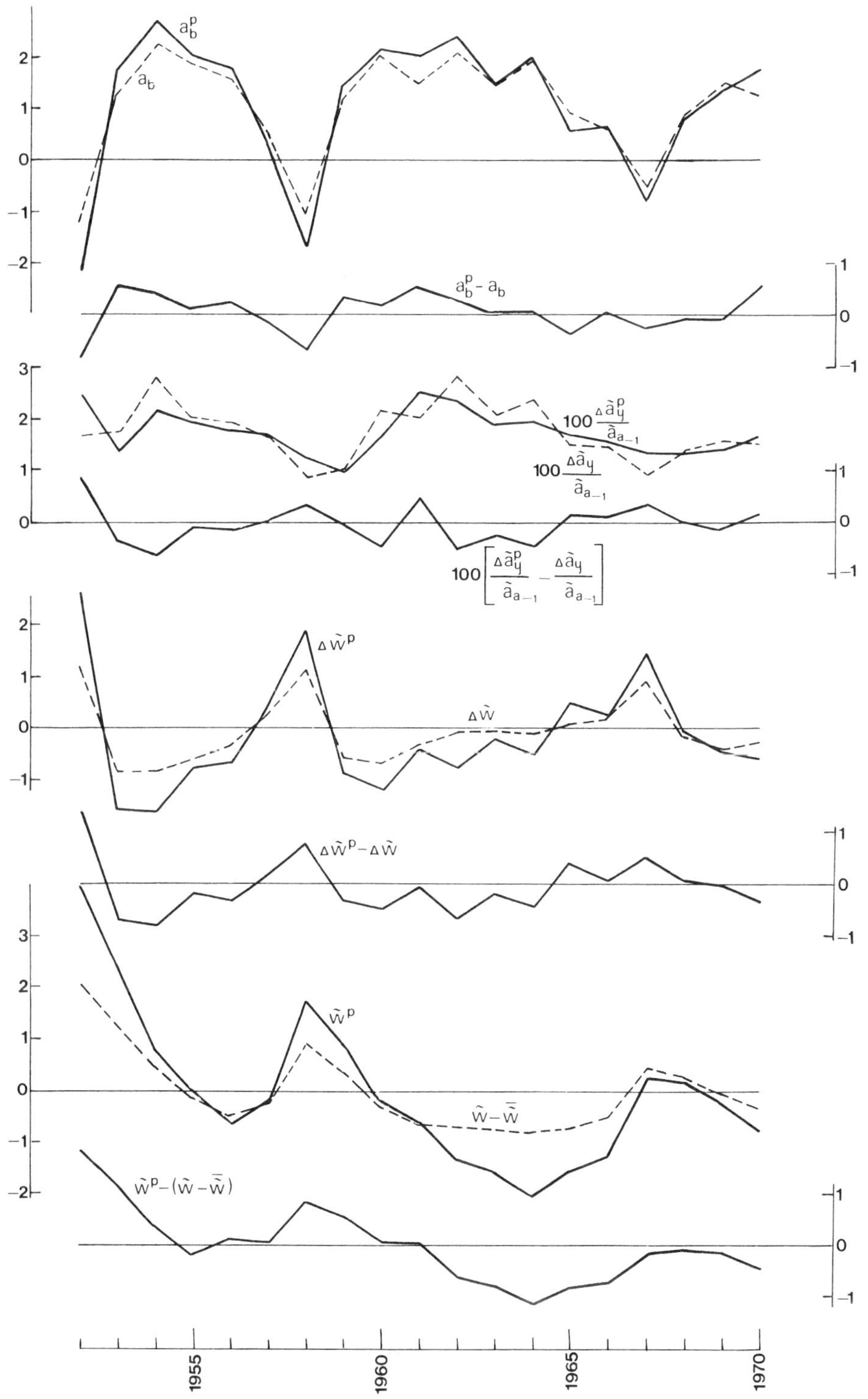

Table 4. Comparison of potential and actual variables[1].

	Potential employment versus actual employment			Potential labour supply versus actual labour supply			Change in potential unemployment ratio versus change in actual unemployment ratio			Potential unemployment ratio versus actual unemployment ratio		
	a_b^{p*}	a_b^f	$a_b^{p*}-a_b^f$	$100.\Delta\tilde{a}_y^{p*}/\tilde{a}_{a_{-1}}$	$100.\Delta\tilde{a}_y^f/\tilde{a}_{a_{-1}}$	$100.\frac{\Delta\tilde{a}_y^{p*}-\Delta\tilde{a}_y^f}{\tilde{a}_{a_{-1}}}$	$\Delta\tilde{w}^{p*}$	$\Delta\tilde{w}^f$	$\Delta\tilde{w}^{p*}-\Delta\tilde{w}^f$	$\tilde{w}^{p*}$	$\tilde{w}^f-\bar{\tilde{w}}^f$	$\tilde{w}^{p*}-\tilde{w}^f+\bar{\tilde{w}}^f$ 2)
1952	-2.17	-1.29	-0.88	2.49	1.64	0.85	2.62	1.20	1.42	3.93	2.09	1.84
1953	1.72	1.19	0.53	1.37	1.72	-0.35	-1.54	-0.85	-0.69	2.40	1.24	1.16
1954	2.64	2.23	0.40	2.17	2.81	-0.64	-1.61	-0.81	-0.80	0.78	0.43	0.35
1955	1.99	1.84	0.14	1.91	2.01	-0.10	-0.78	-0.61	-0.17	0.00	-0.18	0.18
1956	1.78	1.55	0.23	1.78	1.93	-0.15	-0.64	-0.33	-0.31	-0.63	-0.51	-0.12
1957	0.30	0.47	-0.17	1.69	1.64	0.04	0.47	0.28	0.19	-0.16	-0.23	0.07
1958	-1.70	-1.08	-0.62	1.21	0.87	0.34	1.93	1.12	0.81	1.77	0.89	0.88
1959	1.46	1.12	0.34	0.94	0.99	-0.04	-0.86	-0.54	-0.32	0.91	0.35	0.56
1960	2.12	1.99	0.13	1.68	2.14	-0.46	-1.14	-0.67	-0.47	-0.23	-0.32	0.09
1961	2.00	1.46	0.54	2.50	2.00	0.50	-0.38	-0.33	-0.05	-0.61	-0.65	0.04
1962	2.36	2.06	0.30	2.37	2.88	-0.51	-0.72	-0.05	-0.67	-1.33	-0.70	-0.63
1963	1.45	1.44	0.01	1.86	2.09	-0.23	-0.19	-0.02	-0.17	-1.52	-0.72	-0.80
1964	1.96	1.91	0.05	1.91	2.38	-0.47	-0.49	-0.08	-0.41	-2.02	-0.80	-1.22
1965	0.52	0.86	-0.34	1.64	1.50	0.14	0.50	0.08	0.42	-1.52	-0.72	-0.80
1966	0.62	0.58	0.04	1.55	1.43	0.12	0.28	0.21	0.07	-1.23	-0.51	-0.72
1967	-0.84	-0.57	-0.27	1.33	0.96	0.37	1.50	0.95	0.55	0.26	0.44	-0.18
1968	0.79	0.88	-0.09	1.30	1.31	-0.01	-0.07	-0.14	0.07	0.20	0.30	-0.10
1969	1.35	1.44	-0.09	1.40	1.53	-0.13	-0.42	-0.40	-0.02	-0.22	-0.10	-0.12
1970	1.76	1.20	0.56	1.69	1.51	0.18	-0.55	-0.23	-0.32	-0.77	-0.33	-0.44
Mean value	1.06	1.01	0.05	1.73	1.75	-0.03	-0.11	-0.06	-0.05	0.00	0.00	0.00
Variance	1.70	0.98	0.14	0.17	0.29	0.13	1.18	0.34	0.28	2.07	0.56	0.52

1) Symbols are explained in the list of symbols .

firmed by our results. The following regression equations may serve as an additional illustration:[1] [2]

$\Delta\tilde{w}^{p*} = 1.80\ \Delta\tilde{w}^{f}$	VAR U	R^2	DW
(17.5)	0.070	0.943	2.120
$\tilde{w}^{p*} = 1.87\ (\tilde{w}^{f} - 1.52)$	VAR U	R^2	DW
(19.6)	0.097	0.955	0.669

Although the choice of our assumptions is to some extent deliberate it seems to result from our analysis that during the sixties potential unemployment was lower than actual unemployment, while the reverse held for earlier years.
In conslusion, we may state that the estimation results seem largely in accordance with a priori notions.

1. Insignificant constants were suppressed.
2. $\tilde{w} = 1.52$.

8. Suggestions for further research

It would be interesting to use the potential unemployment figures instead of actual unemployment figures in cases where the tension on the labour market have to be represented, such as the Phillips-curve analysis of wage determination. From the point of view of overall macro-economic disequilibrium analysis the integration of this type of disequilibrium labour market analysis with some kind of disequilibrium analysis for the product market - e.g. along the lines followed earlier by the second author - seems important.

The results of our labour demand estimation offer an interesting starting point for the estimation of production capacity. It seems likely that disequilibrium analysis may be a necessary condition for the integration of theoretical demand and supply analysis with empirical macro-economic research. It is interesting to note that the macro-economic models generated by a straightforward application of the analytical principles we used in this study differ substantially from models used so far. Instead of the common procedure in which product demand determines the level of activity almost completely either by itself or corrected for some additional utilisation rate or unemployment device, which may or may not generate stable solutions over time, our type of analysis offers the possibility of having activity determined either by demand or by supply and generally by a mixture of both. The mix tends to switch to the other factor if one of the items outgrows the other. It seems fair to conclude that explosions are impossible in such models. It is beyond the scope of this paper to elaborate this problem. Further publications on this and related subjects may be expected from the second author in the near future.

9. Summary

This approach to the tension on the labour market is based on a confrontation of potential labour demand and potential labour supply rather than actual labour demand and actual labour supply. Industry's potential demand for labour is based on a vintage production function of the clay-clay type, with capital-embodied technical progress, a constant growth rate of labour productivity from vintage to vintage and a fixed technical deterioration. Scrapping for economic reasons is assumed to occur if the labour costs for a vintage outgrow the production value. The impact of changes in the utilisation rate, business liquidity, overtime and shortening of contractual working hours is taken into consideration. The determination of potential labour supply links up with data on population growth and population composition and also with economic statistics such as real wages and working time. The impact of the last two components and that of trend factors on the overall participation is related to the level of the participation rate.

The lack of ex ante data prohibits a simple estimation of potential labour demand and potential labour supply. It is shown that a proper set of assumptions about short-term disequilibrium on the labour market and the adjustments caused by this situation permit mutually consistent estimation of potential labour demand and supply by an iterative method.
The disequilibrium analysis developed in this paper seems to be of crucial importance for both empirical and theoretical macro-economics.

Appendices

Appendix A DETERMINATION OF WEIGHTS

The expression for ϕ in the equations for the determination of u_1 and u_2 in eqs. (3.1) and (3.2) makes use of the hyperbolic tangent. This function is defined as:

$$\tanh(z) = \frac{e^z - e^{-z}}{e^z + e^{-z}} \quad ,$$

which is plotted in Fig. A.

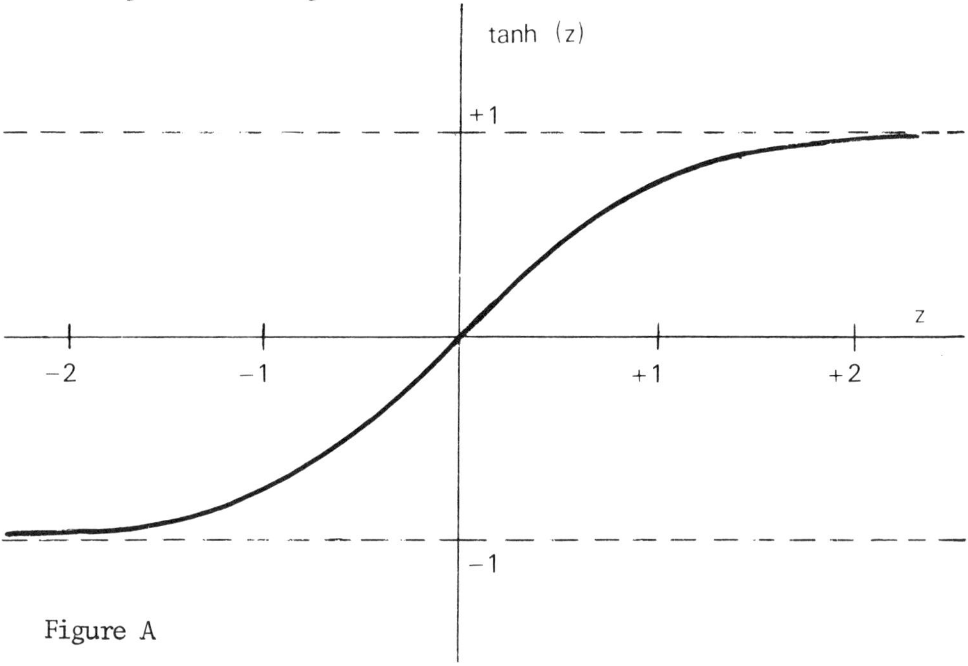

Figure A

Table A illustrated the dependence of the weights on the various parameters. It is clear that an increase in γ tends to increase the dispersion of the weights, while β , δ may be used to influence their mean value. The impact of both α and β on the extreme values of the weights is also demonstrated by the table.

Table A Dependence of weights on parameter values.

This table shows the values of the expression: $u^{*} = u + \alpha\gamma \left[1 - \tanh^2(z) \right] x$

where

$$u = \alpha \tanh(z) + \beta$$

$$z = \gamma x + \ln \delta^{\gamma}$$

$$x = \ln \left(1 + \frac{\tilde{w} - \tilde{w}_e}{100}\right)$$

for different values of $\tilde{w} - \tilde{w}_e$, α, β, γ, δ; where $\tilde{w}_e$ is an arbitrarily chosen equilibrium level.

	$\beta = 0.50$, $\gamma = 10.00$, $\delta = 1.00$			$\alpha = -0.40$, $\beta = 0.50$, $\delta = 1.00$				$\alpha = -0.40$, $\beta = 0.50$, $\gamma = 10.00$		
$\tilde{w} - \tilde{w}_e$	$\alpha=-0.35$	$\alpha=-0.40$	$\alpha=0.45$	$\gamma=5$	$\gamma=10$	$\gamma=20$	$\gamma=30$	$\delta=0.98$	$\delta=1.00$	$\delta=1.02$
3.5	0.277	0.245	0.213	0.365	0.245	0.084	0.025	0.309	0.245	0.198
3.0	0.305	0.277	0.249	0.383	0.277	0.118	0.040	0.345	0.277	0.224
2.5	0.334	0.310	0.286	0.402	0.310	0.161	0.069	0.383	0.310	0.251
2.0	0.365	0.346	0.326	0.421	0.346	0.213	0.117	0.422	0.346	0.281
1.5	0.397	0.383	0.368	0.441	0.383	0.275	0.185	0.462	0.383	0.314
1.0	0.431	0.421	0.411	0.460	0.421	0.345	0.275	0.501	0.421	0.348
0.5	0.465	0.460	0.455	0.480	0.460	0.421	0.382	0.541	0.460	0.384
0.0	0.500	0.500	0.500	0.500	0.500	0.500	0.500	0.580	0.500	0.422
-0.5	0.535	0.540	0.545	0.520	0.540	0.580	0.619	0.618	0.540	0.461
-1.0	0.570	0.580	0.590	0.540	0.580	0.657	0.727	0.654	0.580	0.501
-1.5	0.604	0.619	0.634	0.560	0.619	0.728	0.819	0.689	0.619	0.542
-2.0	0.638	0.657	0.677	0.580	0.657	0.791	0.888	0.722	0.657	0.582

Appendix B DIFFERENTIATION OF $\ln \tilde{1}^{f}_{d}$ FUNCTION

We assume:

$$\ln \tilde{1}^{f}_{d} = u_1 \ln \tilde{1}^{p}_{s} + (1 - u_1) \ln \tilde{1}^{p}_{d}$$

where $u_1 = \alpha \tanh(z) + \beta$

$$z = \gamma x + \ln \delta^{\gamma}$$

$$x = \ln (\tilde{1}^{p}_{s}/\tilde{1}^{p}_{d})$$

Differentiation with respect to time yields:

$$\frac{d\ln \tilde{1}^{f}_{d}}{dt} = u_1 \frac{d\ln \tilde{1}^{p}_{s}}{dt} + \ln \tilde{1}^{p}_{s} \frac{du_1}{dt} + (1-u_1) \frac{d\ln \tilde{1}^{p}_{d}}{dt} + \ln \tilde{1}^{p}_{d} \frac{d(1-u_1)}{dt}$$

or $$1^{f}_{d} = u_1 1^{p}_{s} + (1-u_1) 1^{p}_{d} + (\ln \tilde{1}^{p}_{s} - \ln \tilde{1}^{p}_{d}) \frac{du_1}{dt}$$

or $$\frac{du_1}{dt} = \frac{d\left[\alpha\tanh(z) + \beta\right]}{d\tanh(z)} \cdot \frac{d\tanh(z)}{dz} \cdot \frac{dz}{dx} \cdot \frac{dx}{dt}$$

or $$= \alpha (1 - \tanh^2(z)).\gamma.(1^{p}_{s} - 1^{p}_{d})$$

or $$1^{f}_{d} = u_1 1^{p}_{s} + (1-u_1) 1^{p}_{d} + (\ln \tilde{1}^{p}_{s}/\tilde{1}^{p}_{d}).\ \alpha(1-\tanh^2(z))\gamma(1^{p}_{s} - 1^{p}_{d})$$

$$= 1^{p}_{d} + (1^{p}_{s} - 1^{p}_{d}) \left[u_1 + \alpha\gamma(1-\tanh^2(z)) \ln \tilde{1}^{p}_{s}/\tilde{1}^{p}_{d} \right]$$

If we define

$$u_1 + \alpha\gamma(1-\tanh^2(z)) \ln \tilde{1}^{p}_{s}/\tilde{1}^{p}_{d} \equiv u_1^{*}$$

then $1^{f}_{d} = 1^{p}_{d} + (1^{p}_{s} - 1^{p}_{d}) .\ u^{*}_{1}$

or $1^{f}_{d} = 1^{p}_{d}(1-u^{*}_{1}) + 1^{p}_{s}.u^{*}_{1}$.

Appendix C APPROXIMATION TO FIRST-ROUND WEIGHTS

If $$1_d^f = u_1^* \, 1_s^p + (1-u_1^*) \, 1_d^p \tag{C1}$$

and $$1_s^f = u_2^* \, 1_s^p + (1-u_2^*) \, 1_d^p \tag{C2}$$

or
$$1_s^p = \frac{1}{u_2^*} \, 1_s^f - \left(\frac{1-u_2^*}{u_2^*}\right) 1_d^p \tag{C3}$$

eq. (C3) may be substituted into eq. (C1) which results in:

$$1_d^f = \frac{u_1^*}{u_2^*} \, 1_s^f - \frac{u_1^*}{u_2^*} (1-u_2^*) \, 1_d^p + (1-u_1^*) \, 1_d^p$$

or

$$1_d^f = \frac{u_1^*}{u_2^*} \, 1_s^f + \left[\frac{-u_1^* + u_1^* u_2^* + u_2^* - u_1^* u_2^*}{u_2^*} \right] 1_d^p$$

or

$$1_d^f = \frac{u_1^*}{u_2^*} \, 1_s^f + \frac{u_2^* - u_1^*}{u_2^*} \, 1_d^p$$

or

$$1_d^f = \frac{u_1^*}{u_2^*} \, 1_s^f + \left(1 - \frac{u_1^*}{u_2^*}\right) 1_d^p \, . \tag{C4}$$

If $u_1^* < u_2^*$

and $0 < u_1^* < 1$

$0 < u_2^* < 1$

it follows that $0 < \frac{u_1^{x}}{u_2^{x}} < 1 .$ (C5)

If the positions of $\tilde{l}_s^f$ and $\tilde{l}_d^f$ correspond with those in Fig. 1 it is clear that

$$u_1 < u_2 \ .$$

If the second-order terms are relatively small we may also assume that

$$u_1^{x} < u_2^{x} \ . \qquad \text{(C6)}$$

Now if u_1^{x} and u_2^{x} are determined by eqs. (3.1), (3.2), (3.3) and (3.4) the functional dependence of u_1^{x}/u_2^{x} on the parameters from these equations must be rather complicated. To short-cut inessential difficulties we assumed that the ratio u_1^{x}/u_2^{x} could be approximated to by a function similar to that for the separate elements u_1^{x} and u_2^{x}. This approximation seems acceptable in view of the large range of possibilities of variation for the functions determining u_1^{x} and u_2^{x}.

Appendix D THE IMPACT OF INVESTMENT ON EMPLOYMENT AS A FUNCTION OF THE AGE COMPOSITION OF THE CAPITAL STOCK

The labour demand function derived in chapter 4 contains the factor

$$\left[(1 + \eta')^{-\tilde{m}_{t-1}} - 1 \right]$$

as a multiplier of the investment ratio. For the computation of this factor both the age composition of the capital stock and the rate of capital-embodied technical progress (η) should be known. For lack of specific information we use the following approximation for the yearly change in the age of the oldest vintage

$$\Delta\tilde{m}_t = \frac{\eta - (p_{1b} - p_y - h_c)}{100 \ln (1 + \eta')}$$

which is derived in the text of chapter 4. ($\eta' = 0.01\eta$) .
As indicated there we replace $(p_{1b} - p_y - h_c)$ by the distributed lag expression $(p_{1b} - p_y - h_c)_{t4321}$ in order to suppress cyclic disturbances. Quantification of the expression amended in this way together with a deliberate choice of values for the level of $\tilde{m}$ in the base year ($\tilde{m}_o$) and technical progress (η) enable us to compute alternative sets of values for the relevant multiplier.
The sensitivity of this multiplier with regard to variations in η and $\tilde{m}_o$ is demonstrated in Table D2 of this appendix, while the underlying changes in the age of the oldest vintage are shown in Table D1.
After some trial and error we chose the multiplier values for $\eta = 4.5$ and $\tilde{m}_{1951} = 25$.
As a direct check on the choice, the effects of alternative values of η and $\tilde{m}_o$ on the regression results were studied.

The consequences of the assumed age distribution on the height of the capital stock constitute an important indirect contraint, as explained in chapter 7.

Table D 1 Changes in the age of the oldest vintage in use

year	$\eta' = 0.05$		$\eta' = 0.045$		$\eta' = 0.04$	
	$\Delta\tilde{m}_t$	$\Sigma\Delta\tilde{m}_t$	$\Delta\tilde{m}_t$	$\Sigma\Delta\tilde{m}_t$	$\Delta\tilde{m}_t$	$\Sigma\Delta\tilde{m}_t$
1952	0.94	0.94	0.93	0.93	0.92	0.92
1953	0.41	1.35	0.34	1.27	0.25	1.17
1954	0.16	1.51	0.06	1.33	-0.06	1.11
1955	-0.01	1.49	-0.13	1.20	-0.27	0.84
1956	-0.06	1.43	-0.18	1.02	-0.33	0.50
1957	-0.09	1.34	-0.21	0.81	-0.36	0.14
1958	0.13	1.47	0.03	0.83	-0.10	0.04
1959	0.47	1.94	0.40	1.24	0.33	0.37
1960	0.20	2.14	0.11	1.34	-0.01	0.36
1961	-0.16	1.97	-0.30	1.05	-0.46	-0.10
1962	-0.20	1.77	-0.34	0.71	-0.51	-0.61
1963	-0.20	1.57	-0.33	0.38	-0.50	-1.11
1964	-0.37	1.20	-0.52	-0.14	-0.71	-1.82
1965	-0.30	0.90	-0.45	-0.59	-0.63	-2.45
1966	-0.25	0.65	-0.40	-0.99	-0.57	-3.02
1967	-0.20	0.45	-0.33	-1.32	-0.50	-3.52
1968	-0.19	0.26	-0.32	-1.64	-0.49	-4.01
1969	-0.46	-0.20	-0.62	-2.26	-0.83	-4.83
1970	-0.67	-0.87	-0.86	-3.12	-1.09	-5.92

where $$\Delta\tilde{m}_t = \frac{\eta - (p_{1b} - p_c - h_c)_{t4321}}{100 \ln (1 + \eta')}$$

$$\Sigma \Delta\tilde{m}_t = \sum_{t=1952}^{t} \Delta\tilde{m}_t$$

Table D2. The value of $\left[(1 + \eta/100)^{-\tilde{m}_{t-1}} - 1\right]$ for different values of η and $\tilde{m}_{1951}$

Year	$\eta' = 0.05$			$\eta' = 0.045$			$\eta' = 0.04$		
	$\tilde{m}_{1951}=20$	$\tilde{m}_{1951}=25$	$\tilde{m}_{1951}=30$	$\tilde{m}_{1951}=20$	$\tilde{m}_{1951}=25$	$\tilde{m}_{1951}=30$	$\tilde{m}_{1951}=20$	$\tilde{m}_{1951}=25$	$\tilde{m}_{1951}=30$
1952	-0.623	-0.705	-0.769	-0.585	-0.667	-0.733	-0.544	-0.625	-0.692
1953	-0.640	-0.718	-0.779	-0.602	-0.681	-0.744	-0.560	-0.638	-0.703
1954	-0.647	-0.723	-0.783	-0.608	-0.685	-0.747	-0.564	-0.642	-0.705
1955	-0.650	-0.726	-0.785	-0.609	-0.686	-0.748	-0.563	-0.641	-0.705
1956	-0.650	-0.725	-0.785	-0.607	-0.684	-0.747	-0.558	-0.637	-0.702
1957	-0.648	-0.725	-0.784	-0.603	-0.682	-0.745	-0.553	-0.632	-0.698
1958	-0.647	-0.723	-0.783	-0.600	-0.679	-0.742	-0.546	-0.627	-0.693
1959	-0.649	-0.725	-0.785	-0.600	-0.679	-0.743	-0.544	-0.626	-0.692
1960	-0.657	-0.731	-0.789	-0.607	-0.685	-0.747	-0.550	-0.630	-0.696
1961	-0.660	-0.734	-0.792	-0.609	-0.686	-0.748	-0.550	-0.630	-0.696
1962	-0.658	-0.732	-0.790	-0.604	-0.682	-0.745	-0.542	-0.623	-0.691
1963	-0.654	-0.729	-0.788	-0.598	-0.677	-0.741	-0.533	-0.616	-0.684
1964	-0.651	-0.726	-0.786	-0.592	-0.673	-0.737	-0.523	-0.608	-0.678
1965	-0.645	-0.722	-0.782	-0.583	-0.665	-0.731	-0.510	-0.597	-0.669
1966	-0.639	-0.717	-0.779	-0.574	-0.658	-0.726	-0.498	-0.587	-0.661
1967	-0.635	-0.714	-0.776	-0.567	-0.652	-0.721	-0.486	-0.578	-0.653
1968	-0.631	-0.711	-0.774	-0.561	-0.647	-0.717	-0.476	-0.569	-0.646
1969	-0.628	-0.708	-0.772	-0.554	-0.642	-0.713	-0.466	-0.561	-0.639
1970	-0.619	-0.702	-0.766	-0.542	-0.632	-0.705	-0.448	-0.547	-0.627

Appendix E. Supply weights.

	Demand analysis				Supply analysis			
	Round 1	Round 2	Round 7		Round 1	Round 2	Round 7	
	u_1^x	u_1^x	u_1^x	u_1	u_2^x	u_2^x	u_2^x	u_2
1951	0.252	0.200	0.228	0.292	0.643	0.774	0.778	0.789
1952	0.024	0.068	0.070	0.179	0.592	0.746	0.746	0.769
1953	0.172	0.127	0.134	0.236	0.625	0.760	0.761	0.780
1954	0.370	0.283	0.289	0.324	0.671	0.788	0.789	0.794
1955	0.533	0.381	0.385	0.372	0.710	0.803	0.804	0.802
1956	0.619	0.457	0.462	0.412	0.730	0.816	0.816	0.808
1957	0.547	0.398	0.405	0.383	0.713	0.806	0.807	0.804
1958	0.252	0.184	0.183	0.267	0.643	0.771	0.771	0.785
1959	0.391	0.268	0.274	0.316	0.676	0.785	0.786	0.793
1960	0.570	0.400	0.414	0.387	0.718	0.806	0.809	0.804
1961	0.654	0.459	0.459	0.410	0.738	0.816	0.816	0.808
1962	0.666	0.542	0.535	0.452	0.741	0.830	0.829	0.815
1963	0.671	0.566	0.553	0.462	0.742	0.835	0.832	0.817
1964	0.690	0.600	0.591	0.487	0.746	0.841	0.839	0.821
1965	0.671	0.564	0.552	0.462	0.742	0.834	0.832	0.817
1966	0.619	0.533	0.526	0.447	0.730	0.829	0.827	0.814
1967	0.367	0.358	0.352	0.356	0.670	0.800	0.799	0.799
1968	0.404	0.359	0.360	0.360	0.679	0.800	0.800	0.800
1969	0.512	0.405	0.412	0.386	0.705	0.807	0.808	0.804
1970	0.573	0.476	0.477	0.419	0.719	0.819	0.819	0.810
α	- 0.45	- 0.25	- 0.25		- 0.10	- 0.05	- 0.05	
β	0.45	0.36	0.36		0.69	0.80	0.80	
γ	30.00	25.00	25.00		32.00	20.00	20.00	
δ	1.00	1.00	1.00		1.00	1.00	1.00	
ε	- 0.0165	- 0.002	- 0.002		- 0.0165	- 0.002	- 0.002	

The computed $\tilde{m}_{70}$ = 21.88, (see appendix D) together with the estimated technical deterioration of machinery (ρ = 2.490) enable us to calculate the capital stock in 1970, which should correspond with the value based on ν_{70} = 1.109, arrived at in chapter 7.

As stated in chapter 7 the difference between the two results is very small. The relevant computation is shown in the table below.

	(1) Volume of investment in equipment by industry in 1963 prices (vessels and airplanes excluded) 1)	(2) $\left[1 - \frac{\rho}{100}\right]^n$ ρ = 2.490 n = 0,1,2....21.88	(3) (3) = (1) . (2)
1948	(0.88) 1.771	0.5889	0.918
1949	2.065	0.6039	1.247
1950	2.334	0.6193	1.446
1951	2.232	0.6352	1.418
1952	1.952	0.6514	1.271
1953	2.195	0.6680	1.466
1954	2.822	0.6851	1.933
1955	3.302	0.7026	2.320
1956	3.876	0.7205	2.793
1957	3.707	0.7389	2.739
1958	2.964	0.7578	2.246
1959	3.475	0.7771	2.701
1960	4.032	0.7970	3.429
1961	4.770	0.8173	3.899
1962	5.117	0.8382	4.289
1963	5.365	0.8596	4.612
1964	6.082	0.8815	5.362
1965	6.504	0.9041	5.880
1966	6.968	0.9271	6.460
1967	7.194	0.9508	6.840
1968	8.198	0.9751	7.994
1969	8.750	1.0000	8.750
	------		------
	95.675		80.011

1) in milliards of guilders (10^9)

The ultimate result for 1970 -a capital stock of 80.011 milliards of guilders in 1963 prices - implies an average age of machinery in use in 1970 of 7.4 years.

It is interesting to check the assumed capital output ratio for 1951 as well. However, there is almost no quantitative information about investment and capital losses during the war period and in addition the data for the years before 1940 are rather uncertain.
Nevertheless a tentative calculation provides over-all support for our assumptions about ν_{70} and $\tilde{m}_{51}$.

Appendix G COMPUTATION OF CONTRIBUTIONS TO AVERAGE RATE OF GROWTH OF POTENTIAL EMPLOYMENT

For a computation of the average contributions of the different elements to the growth rate of potential labour demand it does not seem appropriate to multiply the average values of the terms on the right-hand side of eq. (6.2.2^a) by their estimated regression coefficients. The final estimation equation is a highly condensed relation, which should be rearranged for a proper interpretation of average contributions to employment growth. The basis for this reconstruction is eq. (4.6.4), which may be repeated here:

$$a_{b_{t,t-1}} = \frac{100}{\nu_o}(1-\zeta_1)\frac{\tilde{h}_{c_t}}{\tilde{F}_{t4321}}(\tilde{i}/\tilde{y}_{sn})_{t-1}(1+\eta')^{-\tilde{m}_{t-1}} +$$

$$+ (1-\zeta_1)\frac{\theta_2(y_{d_t}-\theta_4 y_{1a_t}) + (1-\theta_2)\theta_3 - \theta_1\theta_5\tilde{q}_{t-1} - \frac{100}{\nu_o}\tilde{h}_{c_t}(\tilde{i}/\tilde{y}_{sn})_{t-1}}{\tilde{F}_{t4321}} +$$

$$- \rho(1-\zeta_1) + \mu(1-\zeta_1)l_{q_{t-1}} - (1-\zeta_2)h_{c_{t4321}} + \zeta_1\bar{l}_{b_{t,t-1}} - \zeta_2\bar{h}_{c_{t,t-1}} \qquad \text{(G1)}$$

This equation contains overtime elements which complicate the interpretation and do not seem very relevant for a medium term analysis. By assuming $\zeta_1 = 0$ and $\zeta_2 = 0$ we may study the average contribution of various demand factors to potential employment exclusive of overtime effects. Eq. (G1) then reduces to:

$$a_{b_{t,t-1}} = \frac{100}{\nu_o} \frac{\tilde{h}_{c_t}}{\tilde{F}_{t4321}} (\tilde{i}/\tilde{y}_{sn})_{t-1} (1 + \eta')^{-\tilde{m}_{t-1}} +$$

$$\frac{\theta_2(y_{d_t} - \theta_4 y_{1a_t}) + (1-\theta_2)\theta_3 - \theta_1\theta_5\tilde{q}_{t-1} - \frac{100}{\nu_o}\tilde{h}_{c_t} (\tilde{i}/\tilde{y}_{sn})_{t-1} + \rho}{\tilde{F}_{t4321}} -$$

$$- \rho + \mu l_{q_{t-1}} - h_{c_{t4321}} \qquad \text{(G2)}$$

Now the first term on the right-hand side of eq. (G2) can be interpreted as the growth rate of potential employment (in man-years) caused by newly installed machinery including the impact of machine-operating time. Changes in the last item may be isolated by differentiating h_{c_t} with respect to time. This yields:

$$a_{b_{t,t-1}} = \frac{100}{\nu_o} \frac{\tilde{h}_{c_{t-1}}}{\tilde{F}_{t4321}} (\tilde{i}/\tilde{y}_{sn})_{t-1} (1 + \eta')^{-\tilde{m}_{t-1}} +$$

$$+ \frac{\theta_2(y_{d_t} - \theta_4 y_{1a_t}) + (1-\theta_2)\theta_3 - \theta_1\theta_5\tilde{q}_{t-1} - \frac{100}{\nu_o}\tilde{h}_{c_{t-1}} (\tilde{i}/\tilde{y}_{sn})_{t-1} + \rho}{\tilde{F}_{t4321}}$$

$$- \rho + \mu l_{q_{t-1}} - h_{c_{t4321}} +$$

$$+ \left[\frac{100}{\nu_o} (\tilde{i}/\tilde{y}_{sn})_{t-1} \frac{1}{\tilde{F}_{t4321}} (1+ \eta')^{-\tilde{m}_{t-1}} - \frac{100}{\nu_o} (\tilde{i}/\tilde{y}_{sn})_{t-1} \frac{1}{\tilde{F}_{t4321}} \right] \Delta\tilde{h}_{c_t}$$

(G3)

The terms on the right-hand side of eq. (G3) can now be read as the percentage changes in potential employment in man-years caused by:

a) newly installed machinery, excluding the impact of changes in machine-operating time[1]

b) economic obsolescence of machinery, excluding the impact of changes in machine-operating time

c) technical deterioration of machinery

d) business liquidity position

e) contractual working hours

f) machine-operating time

Multiplication of the average values of the elements on the right-hand side of eq. (G3) by their estimated regression coefficients for several periods yields Table 3 presented in chapter 7.

1. The influence of working hours h_c on investment via the capital-age variable $\tilde{m}_{t-1}$ is treated under a). Its quantitative importance is very small.

References

1. A.A. Alchian, Information Costs, Pricing and Resource Unemployment, in Micro Economic Foundations of Employment and Inflation Theory, by E.S. Phelps et al., New York 1970.
2. R.G.D. Allen, Macro-Economic Theory, London 1967.
3. T. Amemiya, A note on a Fair and Jaffee Model, Econometrica Vol. 42 no. 4, July 1974.
4. R.J. Barro and H.I. Grossman, A General Disequilibrium Model of Income and Employment, The American Economic Review, March 1971.
5. D. Baum, B. Görzig and W. Kirner, Ein Vintage-Capital Produktionsmodell für die Bundesrepublik Deutschland, Vierteljahrshefte zur Wirtschaftsforschung, Heft 4, 1971.
6. C.A. van den Beld, A Macro Model for the Dutch Economy, C.E.I.R. Model Building Symposia, New York 1968.
7. Central Planning Bureau, Centraal Economisch Plan, (Several "Vintages"), The Hague.
8. R.C. Clower, The Keynesian Counterrevolution: A Theoretical Appraisal, in F. Brechling and F. Kahn (eds). The Theory of Interest Rates, London 1965.
9. R.C. Fair, The Short Run Demand for Workers and Hours, Amsterdam 1969.
10. R.C. Fair and D.M. Jaffee, Methods of Estimation for Markets in Disequilibrium, Econometrica, May 1972.
11. R.C. Fair and H.H. Kelejian, Methods of Estimation for Markets in Disequilibrium: a further study, Econometrica Vol. 42 No. 1, January 1974.
12. R. Frisch, Prolegomena to a Pressure Analysis of Economic Phenomena, Metroeconomica, December 1949.
13. R.C. Gregory, United States Imports and Internal Pressure of Demand: 1948-68, The American Economic Review, March 1971.
14. S.M. Goldfeld and R.E. Quandt, Estimation in a Disequilibrium Model and the Value of Information, Princeton University, Econometric Research Program, Research Memorandum No. 169, July 1974.
15. S.M. Goldfeld and R.E. Quandt, A Markov-Model for Switching Regressions, Journal of Econometrics Vol.1, no.1, March 1973.
16. B. Hansen, Full Employment and Wage Stability, in J.T. Dunlop (ed.) The Theory of Wage Determination, New York 1957.

17. H. den Hartog and Tjan Hok Soei, Arbeid, Investeringen, Produktiefunktie en Overcapaciteit, Memorandum of the Central Planning Bureau, The Hague, January 1971.

18. H. den Hartog and Tjan Hok Soei, Investeringen, Lonen, Prijzen en Arbeidsplaatsen (Een jaargangenmodel met vaste coëfficienten voor Nederland), Central Planning Bureau, The Hague, August 1974.

19. P. Isard, Employment Impacts of Textile Imports and Investment: A Vintage-Capital Model, The American Economic Review, June 1973.

20. J.M. Keynes, The General Theory of Employment, Interest and Money, London 1936.

21. L.R. Klein, The Treatment of Expectations in Econometrics, in C.F. Carter and J.L. Ford (eds.), Uncertainty and Expectations in Economics, Essays in Honour of G.L.S. Shackle, Oxford 1972.

22. A. Knoester, Een Stelsel Monetaire Vergelijkingen ten behoeve van een Empirisch Macro-Model voor Nederland, Maandschrift Economie, July 1974.

23. A. Knoester en P. Buitelaar, De Interacties tussen de Monetaire en de Reële Sektor in een Empirisch Macro-Model voor Nederland, Maandschrift Economie, July 1975.

24. J. Kornai, Anti-Equilibrium, Amsterdam 1971.

25. A. Leijonhufvud, On Keynesian Economics and The Economics of Keynes, New York, 1972.

26. P.D. van Loo, A Monetary Submodel for the Dutch Economy, De Economist, Vol 2, 1974.

27. R.E. Lucas Jr. and L.A. Rapping, Real Wages, Employment and Inflation, Journal of Political Economy, 77, September/October 1969.

28. G.S. Maddala and F.D. Nelson, Maximum Likelihood Methods for Models of Markets in Disequilibrium, Econometrica Vol 42, No. 6, November 1974.

29. R.R. Nelson and S.G. Winter, Neoclassical vs. Evolutionary Theories of Economic Growth, Critique and Prospective, The Economic Journal, December 1974.

30. D. Patinkin, Money, Interest and Prices, Second Edition, New York 1965.

31. D.J. Ott, A.F. Ott and J.H. Yoo, Macro-Economic Theory, New York 1975.

32. A.W. Phillips, The Relation between Unemployment and the Rate of Change of Money Wage Rates in the United Kingdom, 1861-1957, Economica XXV, November 1958.

33. J.C. Siebrand, Potential Demand and External Trade, De Economist, 120, Vol 3, 1972.

34. R. Stone, Demographic Accounting and Model-building O.E.C.D., Paris 1971.

35. R.M. Solow, J.J. Tobin, C.C. van Weizsäcker and M. Yaari Neo-classical Growth with Fixed Factor Proportions, Review of Economic Studies, XXXIII(2), 94, 1966.

36. H.R. Varian, On Persistent Disequilibrium, Journal of Economic Theory, Vol 10, No. 2, April 1975.

37. P.J. Verdoorn, The Short-term Model of the Central Planning Bureau and its Forecasting Performance (1953-1963), in Macro-Economic Models for Planning and Policy-making, U.N. Publication 1967.

38. P.J. Verdoorn and J.J. Post, Capacity and Short-term Multipliers, in P.E. Hart, G. Mills and J.K. Whitaker(eds.), Econometric Analysis for National Economic Planning, London 1964.

39. P.J. Verdoorn, J.J. Post and S.S. Goslinga, The 1969 Re-estimation of the Annual Model (69-C), Memorandum of the Central Planning Bureau, The Hague, January 1970.

40. A.S.W. de Vries, Een Fixed Coefficients Vintage Model voor Nederland, Erasmus University Rotterdam, Institute Economic Research, Discussion Paper Series No. 74.1, 1974.

41. D. van der Werf, De Westduitse Economie in Vijftien Vergelijkingen, Amsterdam 1971.

LIST OF SYMBOLS

General:

1) Lower-case letters stand for quantities in terms of constant prices or price variables.

2) Greek letters indicate coefficients

3) Letters with a swung dash (∿) denote levels of variables.

4) Letters without a swung dash denote (annual) percentage changes of variables $\left[x = 100.\frac{\tilde{x}_t - \tilde{x}_{t-1}}{\tilde{x}_{t-1}} \; . \right]$

5) The use of the symbol Δ preceding a variable indicates a first difference operation applied to that variable $\Delta\tilde{x}_t = \tilde{x}_t - \tilde{x}_{t-1}$.

6) Letters with a bar (-) denote average values; $\bar{\tilde{x}}$ denotes the average value of $\tilde{x}$, $\bar{x}$ denotes the average value of $\dot{x}$.

7) Variables for the current year do not have a numerical suffix. They may or may not have the suffix t.
A lag of 1, 2, ..., n years is indicated by either -1, -2, ..., -n or t-1, t-2, ..., t-n.
A lead of 1, 2, ..., n years is indicated by either 1, 2, ..., n or t+1, t+2, ..., t+n.
The suffix t4321 denotes a specific lag structure
$x_{t4321} = 0.4\, x_t + 0.3\, x_{t-1} + 0.2\, x_{t-2} + 0.1\, x_{t-3}$.
The suffix 0 refers to a base year.

8) In the case of potential variables, 2 suffixes may be used. The first denotes the period for which the anticipation is made, the second the period in which the anticipation is made (Cf. section 4.4.1)
The suffix 60 refers to 1960 etc. Potential variables may also be denoted by the upper index p.

9) Actual values - in contrast to potential values - may be indicated by the upper index f.

10) The interrelations between a number of labour market statistics are shown in Table 1.

$\tilde{a}_a$ dependent working population

$\tilde{a}_b$ employment in industry

$\tilde{a}_d$ total employment

$\tilde{a}_g$ government employment

$\tilde{a}_l$ wage earners in industry

$\Delta\tilde{a}_m$ net number of external migrants with occupation

$\tilde{a}_p$ number of frontier workers

$\tilde{a}_s$ total labour force (labour supply)

$\tilde{a}_x$ dependent working population corrected for frontier workers and external migrants

$\tilde{a}_y$ dependent working population excluding frontier workers

$\tilde{a}_z$ employers, persons working on own account and unpaid family workers

$\tilde{cap}$ production capacity

$\tilde{F}$ share of labour in total income of industry

$\tilde{g}$ working age population (14-64)

$\Delta\tilde{g}_m$ net number of external migrants (15-64)

$\tilde{g}_x$ working-age population corrected for external migrants

$\tilde{h}_c$ index of contractual hours

$\tilde{i}$ investment by industry (in equipment excluding vessels and airplanes)

$\tilde{k}$ capital stock of industry (equipment excluding vessels and airplanes)

$\tilde{l}$ total employment[1] (exclusive of the impact of monetary factors)

$\tilde{l}_b$ labour demand (industry)[1] (inclusive of the impact of monetary factors)

$\tilde{l}_d$ total labour demand

$\Delta\tilde{l}e$ change in employment due to economic obsolescence[1]

$\tilde{l}_q$ liquidity ratio of industry (the ratio of the private holdings of time deposits, demand deposits, call money, saving deposits at commercial banks, foreign currency deposits all held by the public to the value of production of industries).

$\tilde{l}_s$ labour supply

$\tilde{m}$ age of the oldest vintage

m^{x} number of population groups

$\tilde{n}$ non-wage conditions

$\tilde{n}_r$ normal value of non-wage conditions

$\tilde{o}_b$ overtime index

$\tilde{p}_c$ price index for private consumption

$\tilde{p}_l$ wage rate per labour unit consisting of a constant number of working hours per year

$\tilde{p}_{lb}$ wage rate per worker (industry)

$\tilde{p}_y$ deflator production of industry

$\tilde{q}$ relative excess production capacity

$\tilde{r}$ labour force participation rate (corrected for frontier workers and external migrants)

---

1. Measured in labour units consisting of a constant number of working hours per year.

$\tilde{r}^{x}$	labour force participation rate for a constant population composition (corrected for frontier workers and external migrants)
$\tilde{s}$	relative potential excess demand for products from industry
u_1	supply weight in demand-level equation, see chapter 3
u_1^{x}	supply weight in demand equation in relative first differences, see chapter 3
u_2	supply weight in supply-level equation, see chapter 3
u_2^{x}	supply weight in supply equation in relative first differences, see chapter 3
$\tilde{w}$	number of unemployed expressed as a percentage of labour supply
$\tilde{w}_n$	number of unemployed
x	$\ln (\tilde{i}^p_s/\tilde{i}^p_d)$; see chapter 3
$\tilde{y}_d$	industrial production
$\tilde{y}_d^{x}$	demand for products from industry
y_{1a}	difference between the actual growth rate of agricultural production and its average trend rate of growth
$\tilde{y}_s$	supply of products by industry
$\tilde{y}_{sc}$	current supply of products by industry
$\Delta\tilde{y}_{se}$	production loss caused by economic obsolescence
$\tilde{y}_{sn}$	normal supply of products by industry
z	$\gamma x + \ln \delta^{\gamma}$; see chapter 3
VAR U	residual variance corrected for degrees of freedom
R^2	coefficient of determination
DW	Durbin Watson ratio

About the authors

R. S. G. Lenderink is an Assistant Professor in Macro-Economics at the Erasmus University Rotterdam.
J. C. Siebrand is an Associate Professor in Macro-Economics at the Erasmus University, Rotterdam. Formerly he was head of the Structural Research Department of the Central Planning Bureau, The Hague.